UNDERSTANDING WILLIAM S. BURROUGHS

UNDERSTANDING CONTEMPORARY AMERICAN LITERATURE

Matthew J. Bruccoli, Founding Editor

Linda Wagner-Martin, Series Editor

Also of Interest

Understanding the Beats, by Edward Halsey Foster
Understanding Colson Whitehead, by Derek C. Maus
Understanding David Mamet, by Brenda Murphy
Understanding Edmund White, by Nicholas F. Radel
Understanding Gerald Vizenor, by Deborah L. Madsen
Understanding Jack Kerouac, by Matt Theado
Understanding Jim Grimsley, by David Deutsch
Understanding John Gardner, by John M. Howell
Understanding John Updike, by Frederic Svoboda
Understanding Nelson Algren, by Brooke Horvath
Understanding T. C. Boyle, by Paul Gleason
Understanding William Gibson, by Gerald Alva Miller Jr.

UNDERSTANDING

WILLIAM S. BURROUGHS

Gerald Alva Miller, Jr.

THE UNIVERSITY OF
SOUTH CAROLINA PRESS

Published by the University of South Carolina Press
Columbia, South Carolina 29208

www.sc.edu/uscpress

Manufactured in the United States of America

29 28 27 26 25 24 23 22 21 20
10 9 8 7 6 5 4 3 2 1

Library of Congress Cataloging-in-Publication Data
can be found at http://catalog.loc.gov/.

ISBN: 978-1-64336-034-8 (hardback)
ISBN: 978-1-64336-081-2 (paperback)
ISBN: 978-1-64336-033-1 (ebook)

For Jane,
whose beautiful smile, witty charm, and cleverness
have brought new inspiration into my life

CONTENTS

SERIES EDITOR'S PREFACE

The Understanding Contemporary American Literature series was founded by the estimable Matthew J. Bruccoli (1931–2008), who envisioned these volumes as guides or companions for students as well as good nonacademic readers, a legacy that will continue as new volumes are developed to fill in gaps among the nearly one hundred series volumes published to date and to embrace a host of new writers only now making their marks on our literature.

As Professor Bruccoli explained in his preface to the volumes he edited, because much influential contemporary literature makes special demands, "the word *understanding* in the titles was chosen deliberately. Many willing readers lack an adequate understanding of how contemporary literature works; that is, of what the author is attempting to express and the means by which it is conveyed." Aimed at fostering this understanding of good literature and good writers, the criticism and analysis in the series provide instruction in how to read certain contemporary writers—explicating their material, language, structures, themes, and perspectives—and facilitate a more profitable experience of the works under discussion.

In the twenty-first century Professor Bruccoli's prescience gives us an avenue to publish expert critiques of significant contemporary American writing. The series continues to map the literary landscape and to provide both instruction and enjoyment. Future volumes will seek to introduce new voices alongside canonized favorites, to chronicle the changing literature of our times, and to remain, as Professor Bruccoli conceived, contemporary in the best sense of the word.

Linda Wagner-Martin, Series Editor

CHAPTER 1

Understanding William S. Burroughs

A scene occurs early in David Cronenberg's film adaptation of Burroughs's *Naked Lunch* (1991) in which the characters representing Beat icons Allen Ginsberg and Jack Kerouac sit together drinking coffee in a diner booth and debate their aesthetic approaches to writing. The film transforms them into virtual caricatures of themselves as "Kerouac" vociferously espouses his spontaneous prose philosophy of "first thought, best thought" and "Ginsberg" nervously sputters about his need to neurotically agonize over every single word. As the Burroughs character ("Bill") arrives, "Ginsberg" asks him if rewriting truly constitutes a "sin" as "Kerouac" so dogmatically proposes. Bill calmly responds, "Exterminate all rational thought. That is the conclusion I have come to." Bill's response, of course, proves paradoxical because to arrive at a conclusion implies the very rationality that Bill's first sentence so succinctly disavows. Essentially this response, which in no way answers faux-Ginsberg's question, pinpoints the major problems that a reader will experience upon first delving into the universes of William S. Burroughs. Like the philosophy of Jacques Derrida or other poststructuralists, the theoretical side of Burroughs seems, at times, to eat its own tail like an ouroboros as it strips meaning away until a gaping black hole of nihilistic relativism seems to be all that remains in its wake. However, like Derrida's deconstruction, Foucault's genealogy, or Deleuze and Guattari's schizoanalysis, Burroughs's fiction, which itself often functions as philosophy, not only devalues traditional centers of meaning but also offers a new praxis that attacks power at its most fundamental level—language itself—and offers humanity possibilities of liberation. There is, therefore, a logic of sorts to the extermination of rational thought, albeit a new kind of logic for the postmodern and even the posthuman stage of social and human evolution.

As Burroughs always maintained, he wrote for the space age, the age when humanity leaves all its old concepts of civilization, identity, and the body behind to embrace new evolutionary potentials.

Aside from the theoretical implications, the above-mentioned scene from Cronenberg's *Naked Lunch* also gestures toward the almost impossible task of separating biography from theoretical interpretation in the case of William S. Burroughs. Creating a literal cinematic adaptation of *Naked Lunch* would require such extreme sex and violence (as well as the combination of the two) that it would prove incapable of distribution except perhaps in the extreme horror underground—even films such as Pier Pablo Pasolini's *Salò; or, The 120 Days of Sodom* (1975)—a twisted but still tamed down version of the Marquis de Sade's *The 120 Days of Sodom* (written 1785; published 1904)—or Alejandro Jodorowsky's *Holy Mountain* (1973) do not reach the surrealistic heights of depravity that a faithful adaptation of *Naked Lunch* would necessitate. Therefore Cronenberg took inspiration from both Burroughs's novels and his life to craft a still disturbing and gruesome exploration of the writing process, addiction, desire, and control. Like many Burroughs scholars, Cronenberg proved incapable of focusing just on the literary text itself. This study intends to skirt this pitfall into which so much Beat criticism falls: pure biographical criticism. This, by no means, seeks to denigrate the importance of such research, but such works can skew the lens through which these texts are interpreted. A few critics—Robin Lyndenberg, Timothy S. Murphy, Chad Weidner, and Jimmy Fazzino, in particular[1]—have attempted purely theoretical readings of Burroughs with little reference to biography, but among the rather sizeable universe of Burroughs criticism, such efforts remain rare. Several things exacerbate this problem. First, Burroughs's works, particularly his early ones, draw heavily on his life in a myriad of ways. Second, the Beat Generation remains so closely associated with confessional literature (or the roman à clef—a fictionalized autobiography) that it incites a natural tendency to read Burroughs's works in a similar manner. Finally, the vastly different editions of his works, especially the ones from the 1950s and 1960s, seem to demand a biographical explanation of the textual deviations, as Oliver Harris's impeccable scholarship on these texts has demonstrated. While the biographical and archival aspects of Burroughs criticism remain crucial, they can sometimes overshadow the texts themselves and the powerful theoretical potential that exists within them. Therefore this study will take a somewhat hybrid approach that focuses primarily on the texts while still positioning them within Burroughs's life and overall project, for, as Burroughs always maintained, his books all really constitute one single gigantic work. Each individual textual reading will feature a short introductory section that situates the text within Burroughs's life and overall canon and provides details about alternate editions. Subsequently the text will be allowed to speak for itself with only passing references to biography.

Burroughs represents a crucial figure for understanding the various waves of postmodernism that began occurring in the 1950s because his literature, his philosophy, and his life have continued to inspire generation after generation of writers, artists, musicians, and philosophers. Therefore his writings and the persona he cultivated prove essential to understanding contemporary American fiction (as well as genres beyond that). Burroughs's work serves as a bridge between various artistic schools (from surrealism to cyberpunk and beyond), and he—perhaps more than any other author—established the postmodern form of literature and even presaged and influenced the poststructuralist philosophers. Drawing from sources as diverse as surrealism and the avant-garde, hard-boiled crime fiction, pulp science fiction, satire, and the picaresque tradition, Burroughs created a unique, hybrid voice unlike anything before that explores topics as diverse as power, sexuality, language, and identity. While Samuel Beckett's absurdist works and the French *nouveau roman* (new novel) authors were performing similar narrative experiments, Burroughs would push such experimentalism into profoundly new territory where the nature of meaning must be reconsidered on the most fundamental of levels—he would, in effect, break the mold of the novel. Inspired largely by the lectures and writings of Alfred Korzybski, the father of general semantics, Burroughs's entire oeuvre constitutes of an attack on dualistic, Aristotelian, either/or binary forms of thought by using strategies that confuse these simple yet oppressive demarcations. They infuse chaos and multiplicity by always focusing on abject characters that defy the subject/object dichotomy. Ultimately Burroughs hoped to chart a path beyond the evolutionary dead end of the human body. He argued that the human does not represent the apex of evolutionary history but instead is an impasse, a cul-de-sac that prevents the forward progress of evolution. Humanity is perhaps nothing more than basic organic compounds afloat in primordial soup compared to the beings (or perhaps nonbeings) that they might become. Burroughs wanted to take the readers beyond the limits of language and the body and to expand their minds to encompass the infinite; the reader has only to take his hand.

"Like a sheep-killing dog": The Early Years in St. Louis, Los Alamos, and Cambridge

Despite his fascination from an early age with criminals, junkies, and fringe individuals (abject characters), Burroughs hailed from an affluent background. His parents' house was in a gated community of St. Louis. There William Seward Burroughs II was born at home on February 5, 1914. As Barry Miles explained,

Burroughs's father, Mote, was "reticent, remote, rather difficult to talk to," but he did introduce his sons to guns and hunting, thus instigating Burroughs's lifelong love of guns. The women in Burroughs's young life provided a more profound influence on him than his father: his mother and his nanny helped shape and traumatize him into the man he would become. These women instilled in Burroughs a belief in telepathy and the occult. Burroughs's mother, Laura Burroughs née Lee, was rumored to be gifted with psychic powers, and his nanny, who he called "Nursy," began to expose Burroughs to occult spells and ideas. Burroughs claimed that he formed "this hysterical attachment to Nursy" (Miles, *William Burroughs* 22). She rewarded his love with the first major traumatic event of his life. Burroughs went through many different sessions of psychoanalysis (not to mention reaching clear status as a Scientologist) but could never distinctly remember the event. From the evidence his analysts were able to glean, it appears that Burroughs was made to watch Nursy and her boyfriend having sexual intercourse. In addition Burroughs apparently may have been forced into performing fellatio on the boyfriend. Some critics have even posited that this oral rape as a child unconsciously caused Burroughs to almost entirely exclude oral sex even from his most graphic sex scenes. Burroughs never quite fit in and seemed strange to most of his family and neighbors; Burroughs recalled one wealthy man in St. Louis say that he looked "like a sheep-killing dog" (24).

Eventually Burroughs was sent away to school in New Mexico, where he conducted his first writing experiments with an essay he published in the school paper entitled "Personal Magnetism" and a story that he named "Autobiography of a Wolf," which was told from the viewpoint of the wolf, something his teachers could not comprehend—they maintained that it should be called "Biography of a Wolf." Here Burroughs began to fully realize his homosexual desires and was later expelled from the school. After finishing his high school degree, he enrolled in Harvard, eventually receiving a degree in the arts. During this time he also began to visit New York City, where he quickly became acquainted with the gay subculture. Upon graduation Burroughs began receiving his legendary allowance of two hundred dollars a month, which enabled him to live more comfortably than many of the friends he would make later; that is, until he started his junk habit. While he never received any further degrees, he did briefly study anthropology at Columbia University and medicine in Vienna. His studies in art, anthropology, and medicine helped shape his interests from his early works through the end of his life. In fact Burroughs's early trilogy of works (*Junky* [1953], *Queer* [written 1951–53; published 1985], and *The Yage Letters* [1963]) read almost like anthropological explorations that range from the underground world of New York City to the jungles of South America. While in Europe Burroughs met a Jewish woman in Vienna named Ilse Klapper who was attempting to avoid capture by the Nazis. To help save her, Burroughs married her in a completely Platonic fashion and aided her in escaping to the United States, where the pair eventually divorced.

From the Libertine Circle to the Beat Generation: New York to Tangier

Back in the United States, Burroughs's erratic and nonconventional behavior began to worry his parents. Infatuated with a man, Burroughs cut off the top joint of his little finger with a pair of scissors to impress the man—the old Van Gogh kick as Burroughs termed it. After trying to but also subsequently avoiding enrolling in the military (his parents claimed mental instability), Burroughs landed in Chicago, where he worked as an exterminator, an occupation that provided the title for two of Burroughs's publications as well as inspired the character of William Lee in Cronenberg's adaptation of *Naked Lunch*. In Chicago Burroughs became friends with David Kammerer and the object of his infatuation, Lucien Carr. Their antics got Burroughs evicted from his apartment, and Carr's parents sent him to study at Columbia University in New York City in the last in a long string of attempts to get him away from Kammerer, who followed anyway as did Burroughs since he had nothing holding him in Chicago.

In New York Burroughs continued his friendship with David Kammerer, who in turn continued his pursuit of Lucien Carr after his subsequent flight from Chicago and matriculation at Columbia University. Fueled by rebel poetry such as Arthur Rimbaud's *Une Saison en Enfer* (*A Season in Hell,* 1873) and the philosophy of William Butler Yeats's philosophical work *A Vision* (1925, 1937), Carr soon met the first-year student Allen Ginsberg, the son of a poet father and schizophrenic mother, both communists, from Paterson, New Jersey (the home of William Carlos Williams, a major influence on Ginsberg). Ginsberg was attracted to Carr on both an intellectual and a sexual level, and Carr introduced him to the bohemian corners of New York City. During these forays Ginsberg became acquainted with Kammerer and his friend William S. Burroughs. Eventually Carr brought Jack Kerouac, a former Columbia student and football player who had already written several unpublished novels, into the group. With the addition of Kerouac, the so-called Libertine Circle was complete, but the relationship between Kammerer and Carr set the group on a path toward tragedy from the beginning.

Carr and company helped the studious, shy Ginsberg emerge from his shell, and the group began truly living the bohemian lifestyle: drinking in bars, wandering the night, experimenting with drugs, and debating their new philosophy and theory of art. Burroughs remained more on the fringe of the group because he was older and more withdrawn, but his role in the fate of the Libertine Circle would prove essential. Eventually Kammerer's adoration for Carr reached stalker levels, and he repeatedly attempted to lure Carr into sexual intercourse despite Carr's heterosexuality. Finally, on one ill-starred night, the two got into a drunken argument in Riverside Park, and Carr stabbed Kammerer with his boy scout knife. Carr arrived at Burroughs's door and recounted the events of the murder. Burroughs urged him to confess to the police and try to get off on an honor killing plea. Instead Carr found Kerouac, and the two spent the day going to the movies, among other activities, before Carr finally turned himself into the police. Carr was arrested for manslaughter, and Burroughs and Kerouac were picked up for abetting the murderer. Burroughs was lucky enough to have wealthy parents who bailed him out.

During his Libertine Circle phase, Burroughs also met a woman named Joan Vollmer, a roommate of Edie Parker, who became Kerouac's first wife. The two's apartment became a run-down salon of sorts for the emerging Beat Generation and was the location for many of their meetings, in which Joan often played a pivotal role. Still not at home with his sexuality, Burroughs eventually sparked up a relationship with the smart, witty young woman, and the pair lived together long enough to become common-law married and to sire a son: William S. Burroughs Jr., who was already doomed while in utero to a lifetime of addiction, pain, and loss. While living in New York, both Burroughs and Vollmer became drug addicts, Burroughs to morphine (and other opiates) and Joan to Benzedrine, a methamphetamine available in the form of inhalers that needed no prescription—William S. Burroughs Jr. was born addicted to Benzedrine. Wanting to embrace his relationship with Joan, Burroughs traveled to Mexico to get an official divorce from Klapper. During his absence Vollmer had a psychotic break, which did not prove permanent, and was committed to the infamous Bellevue Hospital. The worried Burroughs promptly returned to New York and then moved to Texas along with Joan and her daughter, who she had conceived during a previous relationship. In Texas they became a kind of nuclear family as Burroughs tried his hand at farming in the area.

In Texas Burroughs tried to make it as a legitimate farmer but ended up planting marijuana between the rows to supplement his income. During this time Burroughs reunited with his old friend Kells Elvins, with whom he would write his earliest mature work, "Twilight's Last Gleaming." Herbert Huncke came to work on the farm during this time—Huncke was the Time Squares hustler and addict who introduced Kerouac to the idea of being "beat." Burroughs also began taking trips across the Mexican border for sexual encounters with young men, a practice that Joan always overlooked, and he earned himself the moniker of "Willy le Puta," or "Willy the fag."

After Texas the family moved to New Orleans, where Burroughs became a marijuana dealer. His time in New Orleans led to his famous depiction as Old Bull Lee in Kerouac's *On the Road* (1957). Eventually, fleeing arrest in New Orleans, Burroughs and his family moved to Mexico, where the great tragedy of Burroughs's life would occur. While the murder of David Kammerer in his earlier life no doubt affected Burroughs, it was the death of his common-law wife in 1951 that would haunt him until the end of his life. Joan's death has always been shrouded in mystery; it has remained a controversial issue because of the differing accounts of the shooting that were given by Burroughs, Gene Allerton, and Eddie Woods, who were all witnesses of Joan's demise (T. Morgan 194–96). Burroughs had arranged to sell a gun to raise money, and he and Joan had been drinking throughout the afternoon (Miles, *William Burroughs* 57). Including Burroughs's own description of the event, Barry Miles provides one account: "Bill opened his travel bag and pulled out the gun. 'I suddenly said, "It's about time for our William Tell act. Put a glass on your head."' They had never performed a William Tell act but Joan, who was also very drunk, laughed and balanced a six-ounce water glass on her head. Bill fired. Joan slumped in her chair and the glass fell to the floor, undamaged" (57). Burroughs suffered little legal recrimination for the killing, but the event would haunt him throughout his life. Joan's death caused Burroughs to rewrite an early version of *Junky* (originally entitled "Junk" in manuscript) and set the trajectory for the rest of his career's battle with control (57–58). Cutting Joan out of the novel almost completely was one of the changes Burroughs made to *Junky* before its publication. Despite Ace Books' pressure to include the character of Joan, Burroughs persisted in keeping her and her death out of his first novel (Harris, introduction, *Junky: The Definitive Text of Junk* xv).

The events in Mexico left Burroughs with a hole inside, and he became fascinated with a mystical South American drug called yage that was supposed to convey the power of telepathy to the user. Burroughs conducted two different expeditions into South America, searching for and eventually finding the drug, which would become a recurring image throughout Burroughs's works despite the drug ultimately proving a disappointment to Burroughs. On his first trip, he was accompanied by Lewis Marker, a young man with whom Burroughs had initiated a mostly one-sided relationship—Allerton was not gay but engaged in sexual activities with Burroughs at times. Burroughs convinced Marker to go on his expedition to find yage, an expedition that ultimately proved unsuccessful. Allerton eventually broke off the relationship, and Burroughs planned another yage expedition. This time he found the vine and a shaman who was willing to prepare it for him. The drug provided some hallucinogenic effects but hardly the telepathic powers of legend. Burroughs would go on to detail these events in *The Yage Letters,* which were ostensibly written to Allen Ginsberg.

Ultimately Burroughs ended up in Tangier after reading the novels of Paul Bowles: *The Sheltering Sky* (1949) and *Let It Come Down* (1952), in particular. Tangier was an international zone (the inspiration for "Interzone") in which laws were lax on drugs, sexuality, and so on. Tangier seemed like a paradise of open homosexuality, overt drug trade, and acceptance of alternative lifestyles. Here Burroughs made his literary breakthrough as he churned out hundreds of pages that would come to be called the "Word Hoard," from which Burroughs would cull his breakthrough novel, *Naked Lunch* (1959), as well as parts of *The Soft Machine* (1961) and *The Ticket That Exploded* (1962).

Burroughs worked in a frenzied manner, pouring out pages and tossing them around the room, where they lay in a chaotic pile on the floor. He eventually convinced Ginsberg and Kerouac to visit him in Tangier, and the two began to realize the brilliance of the work that was scattered about the room. Kerouac ended up staying with Burroughs, typing up and somewhat organizing the literary disarray. Despite his help Burroughs found Kerouac a bad house guest, who never left his room, borrowed money from Burroughs to get back to the states, and never paid him back. Kerouac also provided Burroughs with the title for his novel: *Naked Lunch,* a name that indicates the moment when everyone looks at their forks and realizes exactly what they are eating. *Naked Lunch*'s publication is a tortured one that, along with the obscenity trial over Ginsberg's "Howl," ushered in a new era of free literary expression. *Naked Lunch* was originally published in France by Maurice Girodias at Olympia Press, which had already published controversial works by American expatriate Henry Miller and English author D. H. Lawrence. Excerpts from the novel appeared in various publications, eventually leading to their seizure by the state of Massachusetts. The novel was deemed obscene and pornographic, particularly for its scenes that involved orgies, hanging to death, and even necrophilia with the dead bodies. *Naked Lunch* was finally exonerated and published by Grove Press, who still publishes it to this day. A genre-bending narrative with no linear plot, *Naked Lunch* blended elements from science fiction, hard-boiled crime novels, and the avant-garde to create an aesthetic that was entirely new. However, Burroughs was just getting started because he would take his formal experimentations to new heights after his move to Paris.

Paranoia and Paris: The Cut-Up Years and the Beat Hotel

While Burroughs had certainly developed his unique style in Tangier, his radical experimental forays in both fiction and other art forms reached their apex during his time in Paris. In Paris Burroughs settled into a boarding house that became known as the Beat Hotel because Burroughs, Ginsberg, Corso, Gysin, and Sommerville all lived here at one or another time during this period. A former surrealist, Brion Gysin experienced an epiphany when he accidentally cut through several pages of newspaper and noticed that the cut sections fit together to create new meaning. Burroughs became fascinated with the technique, and both he and Gysin traced it back to the Dadaist Tristan Tzara, who pulled words out of a hat to create poetry. Burroughs and Gysin would eventually publish three collaborative works of cut-ups and theoretical statements on the method: *Minutes to Go* (1960), *The Exterminator* (1960), and *The Third Mind* (1978)—problems with the illustrations in *The Third Mind* delayed its publication until the 1970s, after Burroughs's cut-up phase had mostly ended.

Burroughs, of course, recognized that just pure cut-ups would not make a compelling novel, so he selected from the cut-ups he created to build his novels. There are a variety of ancillary cut-up texts, visual experiments, and audio experiments; however, the Nova trilogy constitutes the most important work to come out of Burroughs's experiments. The trilogy consists of *The Soft Machine, The Ticket That Exploded,* and *Nova Express* (1964), and, for many decades of Burroughs criticism, this was the accepted order of the series. Contrary to this Oliver Harris's recent scholarship on the different editions of the novels has led him to argue that the works should not be considered as volumes 1, 2, and 3 of a trilogy but instead as independent entities within a trilogy that has no certain order. Harris based this argument on the different editions of the novels and their complicated publication date. The reader can make up his or her own mind about this issue because ultimately it is a moot point since the entire purpose of the cut-ups is to resist linear thinking.

Burroughs experimented constantly with cut-ups throughout the 1960s, producing mostly unpublishable material that he, Brion Gysin, and Burroughs's lover Ian Sommerville (a mathematics student) produced during the period at the Beat Hotel. It was a fertile period in terms of pushing all the boundaries of art, consciousness expansion, and invention. Brion Gysin invented what he called "the Dream Machine," a cylinder with different shaped slits in it that was set atop a turntable. As the turntable rotated the device, the user supposedly experienced visions, consciousness alteration, and the like. The machine altered brain waves and could supposedly allow the user to experience visions without the aid of drugs—the same kind of claims have been made about sensory deprivation tanks. The group also explored the occult and even conducted spells. Burroughs even believed that he was able to use photography to produce supernatural effects—he firmly believed that he had shut down a shop by cursing it. They also conducted audio cut-ups with the aid of Sommerville's background in mathematics and knowledge of computers. Burroughs also came to believe that audio recordings could be used to incite riots by carefully placing speakers with carefully chosen recordings in various locations around a populous area. While the most famous beat film remains *Pull My Daisy* (1959) Burroughs also began experimenting with film—he and director Antony Balch produced a series of films inspired by the cut-up technique: *Towers Open Fire* (1963), *William Buys a Parrot* (1963), *The Cut-Ups* (1966), *Bill and Tony* (1972). The period certainly slowed down Burroughs's publication pace because publishers simply could not figure out what to do with the chaotic materials that Burroughs was producing.

Despite the cutting-edge brilliance of the trio's experimentation, the years in the Beat Hotel also led to a dark side for Burroughs. He developed an intense paranoia in which he believed the forces of control from his fiction were out to get him. Allen Ginsberg found him almost unrecognizable upon visiting him. Furthermore Gysin and Sommerville fueled the misogyny for which Burroughs had become infamous. The publication of *The Job: Interviews with William S. Burroughs* (1969), billed as a series of interviews with David Odier but actually a collection that features essays by Burroughs interspersed with question-and-answer sections, fueled this image of the author, particularly with its essay entitled "Women: A Biological Mistake." Burroughs has defended his stance in the essay by claiming that he is actually a misanthrope—he hates the human species as a whole, and the separation into two sexes constitutes one of the major hindrances to humanity's evolutionary progress. In direct contrast to all feminist theory, Burroughs claimed that society is matriarchal, citing examples of how women control various aspects of civilization. This period ended with Burroughs's move to London, a country he came to despise. Finally Burroughs returned to New York in 1974 at the age of sixty after spending the bulk of twenty-four years abroad.

Punk Icon: The Return to New York and the Bunker

Burroughs returned to the United States as an underground celebrity and eventually moved into an old YMCA room with no windows that came to be known as "the Bunker," which Burroughs adored for its absolute separation from the world outside. Burroughs's affection for modern music remains hard to discern from his various comments. While he seemed cognizant of the current music scene, he often seemed reticent to comment on the music, as if it did not quite fit his old-world style. During this time Burroughs spent time with rock and punk music luminaries as well as artists and directors, including David Bowie, Patti Smith, Lou Reed, Andy Warhol, Nicolas Roeg, Deborah Harry, Frank Zappa, Mick Jagger, Susan Sontag, Bill Wyman, Joe Strummer, Jean-Michel Basquiat, and many others. Of these meetings, which Victor Bockris frequently put together, several remain more important than others: those with David Bowie, Lou Reed, and, most important, Patti Smith. Bockris published a collection of these discussion between Burroughs and other celebrities in a book entitled *With William Burroughs: A Report from the Bunker* (1981). Burroughs became a huge influence on the burgeoning punk scene. Whereas the beats and the hippies sought revolution through mellow and often pacifist means, punk rock gave zero fucks about who they offended and introduced a level of violence into their music and their shows that had never been encountered before. Partly through his relationship with Joe Strummer from the Clash, Burroughs came to be referred to as "the godfather of punk."

While Burroughs was meeting these celebrities, his writing became more fertile than it had been since the late 1950s and early 1960s. He was churning out hundreds of pages that were eventually edited down into what many consider to be his magnum opus: the Red Night trilogy. Consisting of *Cities of the Red Night* (1981), *The Place of Dead Roads* (1983), and *The Western Lands* (1987), the trilogy is considered by many to be his swan song because it seemed to push into radical new territory while also recapturing everything that he had written up until that point. It was the series of books that seemed to prove his point that all his books were actually one book and that this was its capstone. This is untrue, but the trilogy does include his last three major literary works. Burroughs appeared at the peak of his strength as a literary icon in these three novels, and they do serve as a kind of summation of his career. Many of the themes, characters, and plotlines reappear in the trilogy as Burroughs played with some of his old genres (hard-boiled crime and science fiction) as well as new ones (young adult adventure novels and westerns) to create a series of works that are simultaneously new yet always familiar. While his previous novels portrayed the machinery of control and the possibilities for subversion, the Red Night trilogy finally shows the way out as Burroughs urged the reader on beyond the body, language, and time and into a new space of freedom and incorporeality.

Solitary Life: Kansas and the Later Years

Burroughs eventually left the fast-paced, hectic life of New York City for the calm atmosphere of Lawrence, Kansas, where he would live until the end of his life, working with his secretary, James Grauerholz, to run William Burroughs Communications, a company that even had its own office in town. Despite a few sexual encounters, James could not be considered Burroughs's lover; instead he served as a secretary, archivist, publicist, and so on who helped Burroughs expand his brand and make enough money to be comfortable in his old age. In these later years, Burroughs began to focus on painting, even developing a new technique called "shotgun painting" in which he set up cans of spray paint in front of boards or canvases and shot the cans with his shotgun, thus sculpting the painting in an intensely physical way as paint splashed and pellets from the shotgun shell punctured holes into the surface of the artwork. Burroughs had essentially created a new kind of brush, one founded on the type of violence that he always brought to his works. He would tear apart the idea of the canvas as he had torn apart the textual page of literature.

Allen Ginsberg's and Burroughs's deaths occurred within six months of each other, and the last picture of the pair together featured them holding sugar skulls. Burroughs's funeral itself has become the stuff of legend since he was supposedly buried with a gun, his infamous sword-cane, and a packet of heroin. The proceedings were held up as the crowd waited for Patti Smith to arrive and sing at the funeral. Many of his close friends had died along the way: his wife, Joan Vollmer; his son, William S. Burroughs Jr.; Jack Kerouac; Neal Cassady; Ian Sommerville; Brion Gysin; and finally Allen Ginsberg. As Burroughs traveled on to the Western Lands (or whatever incorporeal existence he so adamantly believed existed), he left a legacy as rich and deep as any other major author. His personality, experimentation, and words had shattered paradigms, and he would teach future generations how to demolish them as well.

Influences on William S. Burroughs

Since he was such a voracious scholar, who studied both anthropology and medicine in university settings in addition to his literary and philosophical studies, the works that influenced William S. Burroughs prove far too numerous and disparate to discuss in such a short space, but some of the major figures that helped shape his ideas and aesthetic are worth noting. From satire and surrealism to sci-fi novels and B-movies, Burroughs's writing—even when he was not explicitly performing cut-ups—acts like a cut-up machine that grinds together elements that run the gamut of human thought and artistic endeavor: hard-boiled crime fiction, science fiction, Reichean psychology, Scientology (for a brief time), Korzybski's semantics, and surrealism are blended together into a razor-sharp amalgam that is often equal parts fiction, philosophy, and comedy.

Above all else Burroughs was a writer of satire, a genre that can be traced back to at least Aristophanes, whose *Lysistrata* (411 B.C.) does not seem too far removed from Burroughs with its throbbing phalluses and battles of the sexes. The genre of satire is divided into three classes: Horatian, Juvenalian, and Menippean. Horatian satire remains tame and good-natured like Alexander Pope's "The Rape of the Lock" (1712) while Juvenalian satire is more savage: works such as Voltaire's *Candide* (1759) or Jonathan Swift's works (*A Modest Proposal* [1729], *Gulliver's Travels* [1726], and *The Tale of a Tub* [1704]) feature a more barbed, take-no-prisoners approach to ridicule. The twentieth century certainly upped the ante on such dark and brutal forms of satire with Burroughs certainly being at the forefront. Burroughs satirized almost every aspect of humanity because, like Swift's, his worldview was inherently misanthropic. Most of the century's dystopian works (Yevgeny Zamyatin's *We* [1924], Franz Kafka's *The Trial* [1925], Aldous Huxley's *Brave New World* [1932], George Orwell's *Nineteen Eighty-Four* [1949], Ray Bradbury's *Fahrenheit 451* [1953], Walter Miller's *A Canticle for Leibowitz* [1959], Kurt Vonnegut's "Harrison Bergeron" [1961], and Anthony Burgess's *A Clockwork Orange* [1962] and *The Wanting Seed* [1962]) featured blunt critiques of power, fascism, and conformity. Burgess's *A Clockwork Orange* and Stanley Kubrick's 1972 eponymous film adaptation certainly set a new standard (outside of Burroughs's work, of course) for depicting a crumbling society clinging to a fascistic structure as many citizens devolve into atavistic gang members, delighting in random acts of violence, murder, and rape (and classical music in the case of its narrator, Alex). A love of music also plays a major part for another important character in the history of satire: Patrick Bateman, an aficionado of superficial 1980s pop music. Bateman serves as the charismatic and funny but ultimately depthless first-person narrator of Bret Easton Ellis's notorious masterpiece *American Psycho* (1991). Ellis's novel perhaps attains another level of the postmodern because it does not focus on the abject as Burroughs did; instead it follows the life of a successful investment banker experiencing the affluence of 1980s New York's upper crust, a space awash in cash, cocaine, and sex. In addition to his mundane activities, Patrick also begins describing his nighttime activities that involve murder and torture. Essentially Ellis's novel concerns how the abject can dwell behind the simulacrum of an Armani suit, a $200 haircut, a perfect font on a business card, and Oliver Peoples sunglasses. As Bateman butchers his victims in gruesome detail that puts most horror fiction and films to shame, he strips away the final simulacrum of the body (as Burroughs so adamantly desires to do). Of course Bateman does not find transcendence in demolishing the body—he only finds the gore that begins to stack up on him. The novel's finale leaves the reader wondering whether the murders happened or whether they were simply delusions—simulacra produced by the chemicals of a disordered brain. Somehow the second option proves even more unsettling because it not only portrays the basest impulses of humanity's id but also calls into question the very nature of human perception. *American Psycho* concerns the very reality film that Burroughs postulated in his Nova trilogy, a reality film that controls and manipulates normal perceptions of reality to ensure that people's actions adhere to the script even if they deviate from what they perceive reality to be.

Burroughs's earliest works were also influenced by the hard-boiled crime novel that rose to prominence in the 1930s, 1940, and 1950s with authors such as Dashiell Hammett, Raymond Chandler, Mickey Spillane, Jim Thompson, and James M. Cain. Private detectives, such as Sam Spade, Philip Marlowe, and Mike Hammer, were a staple of the hard-boiled genre. These characters were able to operate outside the law while still maintaining a certain streetwise code of ethics similar to the Johnson code that Burroughs elucidated in his later fiction. They often disliked police as much as the criminals because they were always shaking them down for information and potential evidence because the private detectives, not hampered by due process or red tape, could more readily access the criminal underworld. Femme fatales constituted another common feature of the genre, women who earned the trust of male characters by manipulating their desire only to eventually turn on them to pursue their own selfish agendas. The novels feature all manner of criminals from thieves to murderers to pornographers. The hard-boiled style gave birth to film noir, a vital, stylistic, and influential genre of American cinema that reached its zenith in the 1940s, only to be resurrected in France with the *nouveau vague* (New Wave) obsession with American cinema, particularly in the films of Jean-Luc Godard and Jean-Pierre Melville.

Burroughs and the Beats were heavily influenced by a string of controversial French authors that stretched from Charles Baudelaire and Arthur Rimbaud to Ferdinand-Louise Céline and Jean Genet. Many of the other Beats gravitated to Rimbaud, whose libertine—almost crazed behavior—and violently passionate views toward life and poetry inspired the Beats. While he remains most famous for his long poem *A Season in Hell* (1873), his second most famous work was his very life: his tortured relationship with poet Paul Verlaine, his radical behavior, and the fact that he entirely quit writing at the young age of twenty-one. Rimbaud traveled until his death at the young age of thirty-seven. While some would maintain that Flaubert gave birth to modernism, it can be argued that it was Baudelaire with his erotic poems and descriptions of the seedy city streets that mark him as the first true modernist. His poetry collection *Les fleurs de mal* (1857) remains a powerful, hauntingly sensual, and provocative experience to any young student of poetry. However, while Burroughs was undoubtedly influenced by Rimbaud and Baudelaire, his major French inspirations lay elsewhere in the realm of the novel.

It was André Gide, Louise-Ferdinand Céline, and Jean Genet who fascinated Burroughs most with their mix of fiction and autobiography and their satirical, pessimistic styles. Writing right after the turn of the century, André Gide achieved fame with his novel *The Immoralist* (1902), which follows a man who falls ill shortly after the start of his honeymoon in Tunisia with his wife.

Gide was one of the first modernists to begin challenging heteronormativity by depicting homosexuality in a positive light. Along with Gide, Thomas Mann's "Death in Venice" (1912), Djuna Barnes's *Nightwood* (1936), Christopher Isherwood's *Berlin Stories* (1945), Truman Capote's *Other Voices, Other Rooms* (1948), Patricia Highsmith's *The Price of Salt* (1952), James Baldwin's *Giovanni's Room* (1956), and John Rechy's *City of Night* (1963) all began to explore sexuality to one degree or another (some more clandestinely than others). These writers were publishing their works as Burroughs was slowly rising to fame with *Naked Lunch* and other openly queer works; however, it was Gide's *The Immoralist* that remained so important to him. Gide's novel tells the story of a man who renounces traditional morality, a theme undoubtedly influenced by Friedrich Nietzsche's *On the Genealogy of Morality* (1887), and one that would influence Burroughs's own conceptualization of alternative forms of ethics.

Even more important than Gide, the open sexuality and squalidness of Jean Genet and dark wit of Louis-Ferdinand Céline directly jived with Burroughs's own personality and sense of humor. Jean Genet's first novel, *Our Lady of the Flowers* (1943), draws on Genet's own life on the streets of Paris and his dealings with homosexuals, drag queens, and criminals. Genet was imprisoned numerous times for theft and other petty crimes. During part of his prison time, Genet wrote *Our Lady of the Flowers,* only to have it destroyed by prison guards. He rewrote the entire novel on toilet paper and managed to smuggle it out of prison. As with Henry Miller's poetically graphic sex scenes, Genet subscribed to a depiction of sexuality that appealed to Burroughs; however, Burroughs would take it into much darker territory with *Naked Lunch.*

Céline's *Voyage au bout de la nuit* (*Journey to the End of the Night,* 1932) and *Mort à crédit* (*Death on the Installment Plan,* 1936) serve as companion pieces. They constitute a twin assault on not just the novel form but on the idea of art itself. To say that they participate in the history of the "grotesque," is an understatement. Filled with pitch-black comedy and misanthropic distrust of authority and people in general in a manner akin to Burroughs, Céline's two most famous novels depict not just war but the everyday suffering of the poor that goes unnoticed by the upper echelons of society. Many would characterize Céline's attitude as "bitter," and this is perhaps true, but his real point is to drag the reader through the muck and mire that undergirds the shiny veneer of society—he takes the reader on a journey with the bugs that dwell beneath the utopian 1950s-esque suburbia at the opening of David Lynch's *Blue Velvet* (1986).

American expatriate author Paul Bowles provided another strong influence on Burroughs, and his first two novels *The Sheltering Sky* and *Let It Come Down* enticed Burroughs to visit Tangier. Bowles lived over half his life in

Tangier with his wife, Jane Bowles, but he had homosexual tendencies that were apparent to everyone despite his heterosexual marriage to Jane Bowles, who was an accomplished author as well. *The Sheltering Sky* follows a married couple on their journey into darkness in north Africa. As a kind of existential dread seeps in to the couple, their marriage begins to flounder, and the novel evokes a profound sense of loss and despair in the reader. While *The Sheltering Sky* takes place in northern Africa, *Let It Come Down*'s narrative unfolds in Tangier itself. The novel takes its title from Shakespeare's *Macbeth,* and it would become a refrain throughout Burroughs's novels, simultaneously referencing Shakespeare and Bowles. The main character's explorations of the International Zone's brothels and underground drug culture directly led to Burroughs deciding that Tangier provided the perfect opportunity for him to escape the trail of crimes and guilt that lay behind him in the United States. Although Bowles led Burroughs to Tangier, it was Denton Welch who Burroughs consistently claimed was his biggest influence. Born in Shanghai to English and American parents, Welch was an author who specialized in fictionalized autobiography like that of the Beat Generation. While his legacy remains less impressive than other authors in this list, Burroughs always maintained his major influence and even dedicated *The Place of Dead Roads* to him. Like Céline, Gide, and Genet, Welch drew from his own life, creating several roman à clefs. Novels such as *In Youth Is Pleasure* (1944) and *I Left My Grandmother* (written 1943; published 1958) are detailed accounts of a sensitive child, reminiscent of the narrator in Proust's multivolume *À la recherche du temps perdu* (*In Search of Lost Time,* 1913–27) and of Burroughs himself, and his experience of the wonders that world around him presents. *A Voice from a Cloud* (1950) describes his traumatic experience of a bicycle accident afterward. His detailed account of everything from the wreck itself to the relief of a catheter provide an introspective account of how one deals with trauma and how it shapes one's future identity. Like Burroughs's other favorite authors (Céline, Genet, Gide), Welch holds nothing back in his depiction of himself in all its wounded fragility and intellectual wonder.

While Burroughs worked on his cut-up novels, other authors had also begun working along similar yet distinct lines. The Nova trilogy constitutes a direct attack on the novel form, but some authors had already begun this battle. It is apropos that Burroughs should be a novelist since his body of work constitutes an all-out assault on modernity, and the novel is the modern genre par excellence. James Joyce may not be a major influence on Burroughs, but his final novel, *Finnegans Wake* (1939) seemed to bring experimentation with the novel form to its ultimate conclusion—for many it represents the height of modernist literary experimentation if not the beginning of postmodern literature. Joyce originally wanted the novel to be spirally bound, so it could be entered at any point; however, he settled for opening the novel in the midsentence and closing it with the sentence's opening. Fellow Irish expatriate Samuel Beckett also experimented along similar lines. He remains most famous for his absurdist plays (*Waiting for Godot* [1953] and *Endgame* [1957]), but his novel trilogy (*Malloy* [1951], *Malone Dies* [1951], and *The Unnamable* [1953]) starts off like absurdist fiction but proceeds to deconstruct the very nature of not just the novel but of narrative itself.

While Burroughs was not directly influenced by them, the *nouveau roman* authors in France were also experimenting with the limits of the novel genre but in a manner distinct from Burroughs. They attempted to create a new style for each novel and often sought to cast off what they saw as the crutches of character, plot, action, and the like. Alain Robbe-Grillet, Nathalie Sarraute, and Marguerite Duras remain the most notable figures of the movement in France. Robbe-Grillet was the spokesperson of the movement with his essay "For a New Novel" (1956), and his works exemplify the aesthetic (or anti-aesthetic) approach to art. In his debut novel *Les Gommes* (*The Erasers* [1953]), Robbe-Grillet dismantled the detective novel by using a technique common to Burroughs—the repetition of dialogue, characters, and narrative until the reader becomes unsure of what happened. *Jealousy* (1957) features a similar technique because it focuses on a suspicious husband who spies on his wife through blinds, relaying to the reader both what occurs and what he suspects until the very nature of reality and fantasy becomes blurred beyond resolution. Together with French director Alain Resnais, Robbe-Grillet wrote the mesmerizing film *Last Year at Marienbad* (1961), a film that, like Robbe-Grillet's novels, repeats itself over and over again. Indeed one could imagine the film continuing after the credits roll in some abstract space beyond the viewers' perception. It is like Burroughs's claim that this book spills off the page in all directions—Resnais's films expand beyond the screen that tries to hold them by deconstructing the nature of time itself.

The Beat Generation

Rightly or not Burroughs receives most of his recognition as one of the core members of the Beat Generation, the nucleus of which formed at Columbia University in the 1940s: Burroughs, Ginsberg, and Kerouac. The New York Beat circle would grow to include Diane di Prima, Amiri Baraka (a.k.a. LeRoi Jones), Neal Cassady, and Gregory Corso. As the group traveled coast to coast across the country, as detailed in several of Kerouac's novels, the New York circle soon was introduced to the San Francisco Renaissance poets, who are often conflated with the Beats: Kenneth Rexroth, Lawrence Ferlinghetti, Gary Snyder,

Michael McClure, and others. The Beats also began establishing connections with the Black Mountain School of Poets, most of whom practiced a form of poetry called projective verse: Charles Olson, Robert Creeley, Robert Duncan, Denise Levertov, and others. While many people lump the Beats, the San Francisco Renaissance Poets, and the Black Mountain School into one giant category labeled as "Beat," this proves reductionary in a manner that nullifies the essential aesthetics that make these groups distinct. Burroughs's ties with the Beat Generation became more tenuous as the group dispersed from New York, and he began living abroad throughout the bulk of the 1950s, 1960s, and 1970s; however, he remained friends with most of these people throughout his life via letters and visits. The Beat Generation authors undoubtedly influenced Burroughs's early works, but he never shared their interests in Buddhism and Eastern religions—Burroughs's spiritual inclinations (if one can call them that) lay more in the realm of the occult—and his works began to fall more in line with the type of artistic experimentation begun by the Dadaists and surrealists.

While Burroughs became more of surrealist, it remains important to recognize the Beat Generation's influence on him and the authors who helped push him into writing. Jack Kerouac persists as the poster boy for the Beat Generation because of the phenomenon surrounding the publication of *On the Road,* a roman à clef that fictionalizes his cross-country journeys with Neal Cassady. Filled with the desire for freedom and self-exploration, copious sexual exploits, and drug use, the novel sent numerous young people hitchhiking in the 1950s and beyond. The novel remains a rite of passage for many budding hipsters or antiestablishment intellectuals in their late teens or early twenties. In many ways, then, the novel often gets read at a similar point as J. D. Salinger's *A Catcher in the Rye* (1945–46), which was published six years earlier, another novel of rebellion but a much more low-key one since Holden Caulfield never manages to rebel in any substantive fashion or even to get laid. Of course, Kerouac and Cassady (or Sal Paradise and Dean Moriarty as they appear in the novel) are older and hence more capable of pursuing their rebellion against traditional American values in favor of the eternal pursuit of "kicks." Kerouac continued to depict the Beat Generation in other novels such as *The Subterraneans* (1958), which is famous partly for being entirely written during a three-day Benzedrine binge and for its depiction of Kerouac's interracial relationship. John Cassavetes's first film, *Shadows* (1959), similarly examines interracial relations during the Beat Generation era in New York and became a landmark of independent cinema. The haunting novella *Tristessa* (1960) depicts his time in Mexico with William S. Burroughs and his love for a morphine-addicted prostitute. Other novels, such as *The Dharma Bums* (1958) and *Desolation Angels* (1965), depict his exploration and final disillusionment with Buddhism.

Burroughs always argued that his works all made up one large work, and the same could be said of Kerouac's works. Most of his works fit together into what he termed "the Duluoz Legend," a fictionalized retelling of his life that ranks alongside of Faulkner's Yoknapatawpha novels and stories as one of the most epic and experimental fictional creations in American literature.

The Beat Generation comprised mostly poets who dabbled in fiction and autobiography at times, but no poet changed the face of the post–World War II world quite the way Allen Ginsberg did. During his time at Columbia, Ginsberg chaffed against the stodgy old poets, such as T. S. Eliot, that were being taught in his classes and instead admired the freedom, individualistic spirituality, and "madness" that he discovered in the works of poets such as William Blake and Walt Whitman. Ginsberg began writing poetry early in life, but it was the publication of *Howl and Other Poems* (1956) as number 4 in the Pocket Poet Series from Lawrence Ferlinghetti's City Lights Books that had such a profound impact on the history of American poetry. The book, like Burroughs's *Naked Lunch,* led to an obscenity trial that helped open literature up to what authors could express. Ginsberg's reputation was further cemented by the publication of what many consider to be his masterpiece: "Kaddish," which appeared in *Kaddish and other Poems* (1961). "Kaddish" is the term for the Jewish prayer for the dead, and in the poem Ginsberg creates his own prayer or homage to his mother, a problematic figure in his life because of her schizophrenia and subsequent institutionalization. In other poems, such as "Please Master" (1968), Ginsberg depicted gay sex in honest and graphic ways that, along with Burroughs's work, would contribute to the free expression of gay sexuality and identity.[2] Ginsberg would proceed to become an elder statesman of literature in the United States, and he helped get Burroughs inducted into the American Academy of Arts and Letters. The two remained friends until Ginsberg's death in 1997, just six months before Burroughs's own demise.

Another major figure in the Beat Generation and in Burroughs's life was Gregory Corso. A fellow resident of the Beat Hotel, Corso published several defining books of Beat poetry, particularly *Gasoline* (1958) and *The Happy Birthday of Death* (1960). His most famous poem, "Bomb," was originally printed as a broadside. A concrete poem, "Bomb" (1958) is shaped like a mushroom cloud and serves as a visceral protest against the atomic age. In a more comic vein, his poem "Marriage" (1960) imagines the first meeting between a young man and his girlfriend's parents and expresses the narrator's desire to act directly in opposition to what parents would expect of a suitor.

When one begins studying the Beat Generation, there seem to be only a few essential names, but these proliferate ever outward as one reads and studies more: Michael McClure, Diane di Prima, LeRoi Jones (Amiri Baraka), Hettie

Jones, Ted Joans, Philip Whalen, Bob Kaufman, Tuli Kupferberg, Anne Waldman, Gary Snyder, Philip Lamantia, Ray and Bonnie Bremser, Ed Sanders, Neal Cassady, John Clellon Holmes, Lawrence Ferlinghetti, ruth weiss,[3] and others. Digging even further the reader will encounter Kenneth Rexroth (the anarchist San Francisco poet who served as a kind of godfather to the Beats) as well as the Black Mountain poets, who had different aesthetic principles but remained closely aligned with the Beats: Charles Olson, Robert Creeley, Denise Levertov, Robert Duncan, and others. Burroughs was not acquainted with all these individuals, but Diane di Prima and LeRoi Jones deserve a special mention because they frequently featured his work in their self-published and self-distributed literary magazine *Floating Bear,* one of the many small journals that published pieces of Burroughs's work. Similarly Lawrence Ferlinghetti would not prove to be a close friend, but he also helped publish several of Burroughs's books, including *The Yage Letters.*

Another major author and publisher of Beat Generation works, Lawrence Ferlinghetti established the first entirely paperback publishing operation in the United States: City Lights Books, still thriving as a designated San Francisco landmark. Ferlinghetti became an innovative poet in his own right with such iconic books as *Pictures from the Gone World* (1955) and *A Coney Island of the Mind* (1958). However, Ferlinghetti remains most famous for City Lights' Pocket Poet Series, a numbered, pocket-sized series of paperback poetry books from cutting-edge authors. The company published many important works of poetry: Allen Ginsberg, Kenneth Patchen, Denise Levertov, Gregory Corso, Frank O'Hara, Diane di Prima, Anne Waldman, Peter Orlovsky, and Jack Kerouac to name only a few. Additionally City Lights published fiction, nonfiction, and other kinds of texts, including several of Burroughs's own works: *The Yage Letters, The Yage Letters Redux* (2006), and *The Burroughs File* (1984, a collection of miscellaneous cut-up works, including *White Subway* [1973], *Cobblestone Gardens* [1976], *The Retreat Diaries* [1976], and selections from Burroughs's cut-up scrapbooks). Like Ferlinghetti, Diane di Prima became famous both as a poet in her own right and as a publisher of underground literary magazines. Di Prima also remains important for her autobiographical and erotic novel *Memoirs of a Beatnik* (1969) as well her major poetic works: *Dinners and Nightmares* (1961), *Revolutionary Letters* (1968), and the multipart feminist epic *Loba* (1973). In addition to her own works, di Prima, with the help of LeRoi Jones and others, began publishing an underground literary magazine entitled *Floating Bear,* which featured Burroughs's works on several occasions. Overall the Beat Generation was a major early influence on Burroughs, but his style quickly moved him into the history of surrealism and the avant-garde.

On Becoming Abject: Burroughs's Blueprint for Defeating Control

Many critics take a biographical approach to interpreting the Beat Generation, which can work with Burroughs throughout most of his oeuvre since he constantly integrates and recycles people and events from real life. However, this methodology proves limited because Burroughs is a philosophical writer in the vein of Franz Kafka, Witold Gombrowicz, Albert Camus, Jean-Paul Sartre, and Jorge Luis Borges. These authors all were, to one degree or another, grappling with the questions raised about meaning and absurdity by existentialist philosophy, and Burroughs starts with existential questions but eventually leaves these questions behind to pursue a much more radical philosophy. Existentialism can be traced back to Søren Kierkegaard, who realized that God's existence could not be proven and that the universe might be absurd. Because the human has free will, he must make the choice of either accepting this absurdity and attempting to live with its nihilistic implications, or he can take a leap of faith and choose a belief in God that makes sense of the universe, hence dispelling the horrors of absurdity and chaos.

In contrast to Kierkegaard, Nietzsche embraced chaos and theorized the possibilities inherent within it. Often mistakenly labeled as a nihilist because of this and his oft-quoted out-of-context statement that "God is dead," Nietzsche actually proposed a new form of individualistic ethos that in many ways extended the critical project of Immanuel Kant without presupposing the necessity to uphold beliefs in morality and god. Aside from this fundamental fault at the core of his thinking, Kant attempted to adhere strictly to logic as he proves the possibility of synthetic a priori statements or his categorical imperative that states that one must "act only according to that maxim whereby you can at the same time will that it should become a universal law." Kant's categorical imperative represents an almost mathematical equation for determining the morality of one's action: one commits an act if one would want everyone else to be capable of committing the same act. However, Burroughs would immediately attack this logic with the question: "But what if a large portion of the populace are shits?" Too many humans adhere to the logic of Thrasymachus in book 1 of Plato's *The Republic* (381 B.C.): "justice is the advantage of the stronger." Of course, as he generally does, Socrates brings Thrasymachus to heel even if Socrates does go on to posit systems of rule and censorship that border on fascistic. Machiavelli asserts a similarly bleak outlook on power in *The Prince* (1532), in which the "means always justify the ends." Kant would challenge this with his second version of the categorical imperative: treat others as an end in themselves. Burroughs would concur with Machiavelli's dim view of humanity and those in power, thus leading him to his Manichean divide between the shits and Johnsons. In many ways the Johnson code adheres to Kant's categorical imperative; however it is more fluid and capable of adaptation.

Like Plato, Nietzsche has also been condemned as a fascist, mostly because of his theory of the übermensch (the superman or overman), which was appropriated by the Nazis as a philosophical grounding for their ideology. This movement was spearheaded by Nietzsche's sister and a careful editing of his notes that were posthumously published under the title *The Will to Power* (1901). Nietzsche would have abhorred fascism because its goal is to transform the population into sheep, and the central purpose of Nietzsche's project is to teach the reader how to cast off slavish, sheepish moralities and systems of thought in favor of embracing the absolute freedom that chaos provides. People cannot trust their morality, ideas, and so on to be governed by "the shits" (the later Julio-Claudian emperors, the leaders of the Spanish Inquisition, Adolf Hitler, Benito Mussolini, Mao Zedong, the Kim dynasty of North Korea, Joseph Stalin, Idi Amin, Pol Pot, and Donald Trump, to name only a few). Shits exist outside the ranks of dictators—anyone who tries to force their thinking on others is a shit. As Burroughs stated, "the mark of your basic shit is that he has to be right" (*The Place of Dead Roads* 155). Nietzsche's concept of the eternal return of the same (or recurrence) resides at the basis of his theory of ethics even though he never exactly espouses it in a formula as Kant provides—a formula remains antithetical to his embracing of chaos, of beginning without any preconceived ideas (on a plane of immanence as Deleuze terms it). Ethics, therefore, resides solely within the individual. To express it in Burroughs's terminology, if one knows that one is about to commit a shitty act, then one should reconsider it.

Unlike the absurdists and existentialists, Burroughs was revolutionary in the fact that he explored the philosophical conundrums that poststructuralism, deconstruction, postmodernism, and posthumanism would later examine in nonfictional formats. He leaves the questions of Sartre, Camus, Simone de Beauvoir, Karl Jaspers, William Barrett, and others behind—existentialism was a modernist form of thinking and even a structuralist one as it sought to create organized meaning in the face of chaos (even if it was only on an individualistic level). Burroughs's earlier works remain existential at their core, but his novels from *Naked Lunch* onward plunge into profoundly new spaces that philosophy had yet to map out. Heavily influenced by Korzybski, his works attacked dualism in a similar way as the major sea change in philosophy that was soon to come—in particular it assaulted the dichotomous, linear thinking of cause and effect. While he came from a completely different school of thinking than Korzybski, Jacques Derrida emerged in the 1960s to launch an assault on not just dualism but language itself. Influenced by the philosophy of Hegel, Nietzsche, Husserl, and Heidegger as well as the study of semiotics inaugurated by the work of Ferdinand de Saussure, Jacques Derrida unleashed three books in 1967 that defined deconstruction and forever changed the face of philosophy and literary criticism: *Voice and Phenomena*, *Of Grammatology*, and *Writing and Difference*. Deconstruction continued to grow as a movement or school of thought through the works of other major critics: J. Hillis Miller's *The Disappearance of God* (1963), Roland Barthes's "The Death of the Author" (1967), Julia Kristeva's *Desire in Language* (1969) and *Powers of Horror* (1980), Paul de Man's *Allegories of Reading* (1979), and so on. Many other authors adopted deconstructive techniques, and the practice often gets used in literary criticism, philosophy, and theory without its name ever being mentioned.

Power remains another persistent theme in Burroughs's fiction. In fact his fiction parallels, presaged, or even influenced structuralist and poststructuralist conceptualizations of power that were formulated by theorists such Louis Althusser, Michel Foucault, Gilles Deleuze and Fèlix Guattari, and Michael Hardt and Antonio Negri. Burroughs focuses on a form of power that he terms "control," a ubiquitous force that infiltrates even the most mundane aspects of quotidian life. The postmodern evolution of power, control is decentered and hence not constricted to any nation or regime. It spreads itself out across the globe and is not directed by any individual, congress, or cohort—it constantly changes form to adapt to changes in subject life and global relations.

From *Naked Lunch* through the Red Night trilogy, Burroughs imagined ways of battling control and its various mechanisms of subjectification. To do so he focused on the individuals that dwelt on the edges of society, trying to exempt themselves from society's power structures. Since his childhood Burroughs had always identified with what Julia Kristeva would term "the abject," those individuals who are neither subject or object because they cannot be neatly inserted into the paradigm of control—they are square pegs that control attempts to insert into round holes. Because they do not fit, they become the marginal, the unnamable, and must either bend themselves into new shapes or accept their abjectivity.

Burroughs always seeks to put himself in out of the abject position both in his life and in his writing from his earliest novels onward. From the abject position, one can achieve new methods of transgression, of fighting control. The abject takes itself out of the regime of power by refusing to accept a defined position within it. As Althusser argued a subject of power must be interpellated into the system, given a place as a subject in both the grammatical sense and the political sense, both of which prove to be intertwined. The subject must be addressable by the system of power just as a person's name must be capable of filling the subject position in a sentence. The abject refuses such interpellation, rendering him- or herself unrecognizable to the control grid. Of course William S. Burroughs exists as a legal entity and can be addressed either in speech or writing; however, *el hombre invisible,* the gay junkie subversive, does not fit into the system—in fact he seeks to dismantle it by attacking the very language structure that assigns values such as subject and object. Since the grid cannot recognize the abject, it marginalizes it, hoping to reduce its infectious qualities. Burroughs seeks to utilize the abject as a staging ground for revolutionary activity. The abject refuses the traditional organization of the body and rewrites it in a manner that defies traditional dualistic, binary thought. In many ways Burroughs's writings seek to reach the body without organs, the zero ground in which all organization falls apart. The BwO (body without organs) equals death, but by stripping thought down to that level, new revolutionary organizations can be created to challenge the dualistic conception of the universe.

"Don't worry . . . I'm the doctor"

The finale on the Beatles' *Revolver* (1966), "Tomorrow Never Knows," a sitar-heavy and dissonant track that presages their more experimental work to come, opens with the line "Turn off your mind, relax, and float downstream." The Beatles' subsequent album, *Sgt. Pepper's Lonely Hearts Club Band* (1967), features a picture of Burroughs in the faux–group shot on the cover; however it is this line from "Tomorrow Never Knows" that provides a perfect method of approaching Burroughs when reading him for the first time. In fact many Burroughs critics suggest that his individual works should simply be viewed as segments in a larger, multimedia project that includes his writings, his paintings, his notebooks and journals, his film and audio experiments, and his life itself. To try and understand every aspect of a Burroughs's text or, even more dauntingly, to try and piece it altogether into coherence will prove impossible. Humanity craves such coherence because it remains trapped in time, in linear concepts of narrative and reality, but Burroughs beckons readers to leave time behind and embrace space, to break free from all that binds their minds to concepts such as capitalism, Marxism, bureaucracy, religion, and so on. Even science itself can take humanity only so far because mainstream, institutionalized science pays no attention to and even attempts to block alternative ideas, such as the occult, the paranormal, non-FDA-sanctioned drugs, and so on. Burroughs bought the ticket and took the ride (to paraphrase Hunter S. Thompson from *Fear and Loathing in Las Vegas*), so readers do not have to—he is the reader's tour guide to the fringe, the marginal, the bizarre, the hellish, and the other. He will take the reader from the mean streets of post–World War II New York to various other realities, possible futures, and states of consciousness. From *Naked Lunch* onward, Burroughs's texts will seem confusing, revolting, pornographic, and possibly even insane. A dark beauty, a hilarious and visceral sense of humor, and a completely radical philosophy permeate these seemingly chaotic pages. As readers encounter more Burroughs, they will come to understand his humor, his point of view, and his purpose. In many ways the readers' letting an academic tell them how to understand Burroughs goes against the very nature of his project, but this humble guide still hopes to provide a serviceable introduction to different ways of approaching the author without ever denying the infinite array of possible interpretations one might derive from a Burroughs text. To approach Burroughs one must adopt a fully postmodern perspective—there is not a master signifier that will give meaning to his works, for these are merely the traces that accrue around the proper name "William S. Burroughs." He is the tour guide down these different paths, and the readers' job is to turn off their minds. If the readers can do that, then they just might experience something completely new. He functions like his character Dr. Benway, who guides William Lee around the various horrors that he has perpetrated on Freeland in *Naked Lunch*. Burroughs has paid for the trip. He is the doctor and has the prescription the reader needs. Humanity does not need to waste their lives waiting for the man or fretting over getting a hot shot; all they have to do is take the ride.

CHAPTER 2

Desire and the Ugly Spirit

Obsession, Addiction, and *Jouissance* in Burroughs's Early Fiction

Burroughs dabbled in writing at various points in his life: he published an essay called "Personal Magnetism" in his school's literary magazine while he was still in St. Louis in 1929, and he collaborated on a piece entitled "Twilight's Last Gleaming" with lifelong friend Kells Elvins (T. Morgan 39–40 and 67–68). But it was the prompting of Jack Kerouac, who had begun writing novels in the early 1940s, that led Burroughs down the path to becoming a professional author. After the murder of David Kammerer, Burroughs and Kerouac collaborated on a novel in 1945 about the Carr-Kammerer affair, but the novel would remain unpublished for six decades. Finally the publication of Kerouac's *The Town and the City* in 1950 gave hope to the rising Beat Generation authors, and Burroughs began writing again. Following Kerouac's lead Burroughs's early works rely heavily on events from his own life: *Junky, Queer,* and *The Yage Letters* received inspiration from Burroughs's time in New York, Texas, New Orleans, Mexico, and South America. However, the novels should not just be read as texts that provide insight into the author's life and mind. Numerous books have been written expounding on how the characters and stories parallel real-life events, but this work will focus instead on how these early works provide examples of Burroughs beginning to slowly hone his own unique style by experimenting with different narrative techniques and exploring the nature of the abject and its relation to the dualistic control apparatus. While these early works differ markedly from his more mature ones and do not feature the signature Burroughs style, they still interrogate what would become one of

Burroughs's overriding themes throughout his career—the relation between desire and control as well as how one's desire can lead to abjectivity. Therefore this chapter will look at how Burroughs's first four novels, *And the Hippos Were Boiled in Their Tanks, Junky, Queer,* and *The Yage Letters*, use different styles and narrative structures to explore distinct forms of desire before then proceeding to a final analysis of certain short works collected in *Interzone* (an anthology of shorter early Burroughs works) that help demonstrate the transition into Burroughs's mature style in *Naked Lunch*.

The Gordian Knot of Desire: Burroughs, Kerouac, and the Carr-Kammerer Murder

Unlike his friend Jack Kerouac, William S. Burroughs never planned to be a writer, and his earliest works developed from the encouragement of his friends and even in collaboration with them. As Barry Miles argued in *William Burroughs: El Hombre Invisible,* Burroughs required collaborators in his early writings, either directly through joint writing or indirectly via the exchange of drafts in letters to Allen Ginsberg. His early works differ markedly from his more mature writings because they participate in a confessional form of literature similar to that practiced by Jack Kerouac, Neal Cassady, John Clellon Holmes, Diane di Prima, Ed Sanders, and others. *Junky, Queer,* and *The Yage Letters* make up a confessional trilogy of sorts based on Burroughs's experiences in the late 1940s and early 1950s; however, before these three books, he wrote one lesser-known novel: the posthumously published *And the Hippos Were Boiled in Their Tanks,* which he coauthored with Jack Kerouac years before either author was actually published. Even this early novel already begins to explore the nature of desire, a theme that will persist in various manifestations throughout his career

Kerouac's and Burroughs's first novels, *The Town and the City* and *Junky* respectively, both constitute impressive debut novels, yet they pale in comparison to both authors' later, more mature and experimental works. While interesting from a historical perspective, *And the Hippos Were Boiled in Their Tanks* proves to be an even more amateurish work. The short novel is a fictionalized account of the Beat Generation's early years, their friendship with Lucien Carr, and Carr's eventual murder of David Kammerer. Although the duo wrote it in 1945, Burroughs's friend and literary executor, James Grauerholz, promised Lucien Carr that the novel would never be released until after Carr's death; therefore the novel did not appear for public consumption until 2008.

Before discussing the novel, it is important to have a basic understanding of the so-called Riverside Park murder because Lucien Carr and the murder had a profound impact on the young Beat authors. The story has been the subject of much writing and critical and historical reflection as well as a cinematic adaptation entitled *Kill Your Darlings* (2013). Kerouac himself wrote about the murder on three different occasions: not just in *And the Hippos Were Boiled in Their Tanks* and *The Town and the City* but also in the last novel he published before he died—*Vanity of Duluoz* (1967). He even reworked *And the Hippos Were Boiled in Their Tanks* into his own short novel *I Wish I Were You* (written 1945), which was only recently published for the first time in *The Unknown Kerouac* (2016). While Carr never became a famous writer like his friends did, his influence on Burroughs, Kerouac, and Ginsberg remains indisputable. Like Burroughs, Carr and Kammerer were from St. Louis, and Kammerer first met Carr "when he [Carr] joined a play group for boys run by Kammerer, who was then an instructor in English at Washington University" (T. Morgan 85). Although he was fourteen years older, Kammerer became infatuated with Carr, whose parents began to transfer him from one school to another around the country in a feeble attempt to keep him away from Kammerer: from St. Louis he went to Exeter Academy in Massachusetts, followed by Bowdoin College, Washington University, and finally the University of Chicago, but Kammerer moved from one location to another to stay near Carr (Blank 22–23). While in Chicago the pair began hanging out with Burroughs, who was working as an exterminator at the time. The three friends often pursued in excessive forms of behavior, and, channeling the antics of Arthur Rimbaud, Carr frequently engaged in public displays that brought trouble to the group. Graham Caveney described one such irreverent event that partially led to the trio's flight to New York: "Wild times were the norm, and eventually Burroughs was ejected from his lodgings when his landlady discovered that the three of them had been tearing up the *en suite* Bible and pissing out the window" (55–57). Another major event that separated the three friends was Carr's suicide attempt: "Carr put his head in an oven and switched on the gas. Why? asked the doctor. Carr offered the explanation that it was a work of art" (Campbell 12). This answer, which again hearkens back to Rimbaud, landed Carr in a psychiatric ward for a month. Afterward Carr tried to escape Kammerer again by enrolling in Columbia, but Kammerer followed him there, and soon so did Burroughs (Caveney 57).

Columbia provided the backdrop for the nucleus of the Beat Generation to meet: Burroughs, Ginsberg, and Carr (T. Morgan 88–89). Eventually the group grew to include Jack Kerouac, a former student of Columbia, who had already written stories, novels, and novellas, many of which would not be published until after his death. The group began calling themselves "the Libertine Circle" and discussing Carr's idea for a "New Vision," a derivative blend of philosophies that was particularly influenced by William Butler Yeats's *A Vision*. Carr eventually began a relationship with a serious girlfriend, and Kammerer became ever more jealous and obsessed, even to the point of sneaking into Carr's apartment to watch him sleep. This escalation culminated in Kammerer's death. While the motives for and the actual events leading up to the murder have been heavily debated, James Grauerholz succinctly described the facts of the murder: "In cruisy Riverside Park on New York's Upper West Side, Lucien and Dave were alone, drunk and quarreling. They wrestled and struggled in the grass, and then Lucien stabbed Dave with his little Boy Scout knife, twice, in the upper chest. Dave passed out. Lucien assumed he was dead and he rolled Dave's limp body into the Hudson River—unconscious and bleeding out, arms tied together with shoelaces, pants weighted with rocks—to drown" (187). During that time Carr visited both Burroughs and Kerouac for their advice, causing them to be arrested as accomplices. Carr's attorneys played the incident off as a so-called honor slaying, a homophobic defense that claims that a heterosexual individual is protecting himself from the unwanted advances of a homosexual man. Carr pled guilty to first-degree manslaughter, was sentenced to a maximum of ten years in Elmira, and was released after two (Grauerholz 189–200). The incident left an indelible mark on the young, yet to be labeled "Beat Generation," and Kerouac and Burroughs's novel represents one attempt to deal with the tragically perplexing incident.

The pair wrote alternating chapters in the book: Burroughs would write a chapter and hand it off to Kerouac, who would provide feedback and write his own continuation. The two never worked to establish fluid continuity, and the novel has a disjointed, amateurish feel to it. As Bill Morgan remarked in *The Beat Generation in New York,* "Fortunately for their later literary reputations, it was never published" in their lifetimes (5). This cycle continued until they finished the narrative, which features a hard-boiled style reminiscent of Dashiell Hammett and Raymond Chandler but that also mixes in elements of existential fiction as does the work of Jean-Paul Sartre and Albert Camus, who had risen to prominence at the time. Kerouac wrote under the name Mike Ryko while Burroughs appeared as Will Dennison, a name that Kerouac would reuse for the fictionalized Burroughs in *The Town and the City.* Written years before any of the other Beat novels, *And the Hippos Were Boiled in Their Tanks* proves interesting because it depicts the early Beat Generation group hanging out together, minus Allen Ginsberg. Friends Lucien Carr and David Kammerer respectively appear under the names Philip Tourian and Ramsay Allen. In many ways the novel connects with several of Kerouac's posthumously published early works, particularly the novella *Orpheus Emerged* (written 1945; published 2002), which concerns the Beat writers' experiences at Columbia University, and *The Sea Is My Brother* (written 1942; published 2011), a novel that depicts Kerouac's experiences with the merchant marine.

In a letter to his sister Caroline on March 14, 1945, Kerouac provided a description of *And the Hippos Were Boiled in Their Tanks,* which he was actively trying to publish: “a portrait of the ‘lost’ segment of our generation, hard-boiled, honest, and sensationally real” (*Letters* 1:86). Here Kerouac situates the novel in the hard-boiled tradition, and it does feature the hard-boiled obsession with drugs, “lurid” sex, and “underground” characters; however it is missing the central detective character or criminal that generally drives hard-boiled fiction. Who is the Sam Spade? The Philip Marlowe? The Continental Op? Is it Dennison or Ryko? Furthermore most hard-boiled works open with a mystery (a missing person, a murder case, or an object that must be found) or (if they are not a detective story) they follow the exploits of a criminal. While *And the Hippos Were Boiled in Their Tanks* may seem to deviate wildly from some such hard-boiled tropes, it functions as a kind of existential, psychoanalytical detective novel in which the dual detectives of Dennison and Ryko attempt to solve the enigma of the Tourian/Allen problem. Over the course of the novel, they will offer their alternating viewpoints on the topic to make sense of the seemingly absurd friendship and to discover means of diffusing the potentially dangerous situation. The novel proves existential because the two competing voices attempt to create meaning from the absurd. As the two voices offer their separate experiences of the events leading up to the murder, the novel depicts meaning as elusive, subjective, and potentially unattainable. The relationship between Tourian and Allen serves as the central paradox because while Allen’s stalkerish pursuit of Tourian annoys him, Tourian still seems incapable of entirely severing the connection, which would be the logical choice. Instead the pair seemed locked in the inscrutable force of a desire that cannot be pinned down to mere sexuality.

The novel opens when Tourian, Allen, Ryko, and Agnes arrive at Dennison’s place in the middle of the night. Dennison immediately gestures toward the magnetic attraction that Tourian exudes over Allen. Dennison describes Tourian as “the kind of boy literary fags write sonnets to” (4). Ramsay Allen, on the other hand, “is a very intelligent guy but you wouldn’t know it to see him now. He is so stuck on Philip he is hovering over him like a shy vulture, with a foolish sloppy grin on his face” (4). Dennison maintains that Tourian and Allen are both “all right,” but “when they get together something happens, and they form a combination which gets on everybody’s nerves” (4). This introduction to the characters seems innocent at first until the reader slowly begins to see the stalkerish behavior of Allen together with Tourian’s hatred of it coupled with his simultaneous need for Allen’s adoration.

Most of the novel concerns the characters’ hanging out and Tourian’s increased desire to sever his relationship with Allen. Eventually Tourian hits on the idea of shipping out with Ryko in the merchant marine, yet he remains locked in a Gordian knot of desire with Allen that can never be untangled except with a blade. Tourian expresses this fatalistic nature of their relationship early on in a conversation with Ryko, who does not really see the big deal: While Ramsay's desires center entirely on a relationship with Philip, Philip's desires lie elsewhere—he harbors the literary-philosophical goal of realizing his "New Vision." Like Ramsay, Philip's desire also remains unfulfilled, and so the two circle each other, seeking sublimation in an object that the other cannot give.

Allen explains to Dennison that he desires more than sexual conquest; he seeks Philip's love and adoration, which, as Dennison points out, seems far less attainable than a mere one-night stand with the young man. While Allen obsesses over an impossible relationship, Philip seems unable to consummate his own relationship with his girlfriend Barbara. The pair engage in amorous make-out sessions even to the point of dry-humping in their underwear but never manage to progress to actual intercourse. The explanation comes on a particular night out without Ramsay, when Philip treats Barbara indifferently, even harshly, and Ryko comments, "I figured that now he had Ramsay Allen out of the way, he no longer had to rely on her" (47). Barbara, thus, acts as a twist on the concept of the "beard," the female companion that certain gay men use to "prove" their heterosexuality to the public while remaining in the closet. Philip uses Barbara to prove his heterosexuality to ward off Ramsay's advances, a strategy that only backfires and drives Ramsay to more extreme stalkerish behavior.

As he resorts to illegal methods to observe his beloved, Philip feels trapped by his current life. In the same chapter as the revelation about Barbara, Philip also opines about the human condition: "You're a fish in a pond. It's drying up. You have to mutate into an amphibian, but someone keeps hanging on to you and telling you to stay in the pond, everything's going to be all right" (46). A few seconds later, the radio broadcasts a report about a fire at the zoo (the actual origin of the title), and Philip responds, "And the hippos were boiled to death in their tanks" (46). Here Philip depicts two different systems: one of homeostasis (one in which the animal remains incapable of change) and another of transistasis, in which life forms adapt to changes in their environment. Philip's relationship mirrors his literary and philosophical ambitions, another empty facade that he makes plenty of noise about in public without generating any actual work to show for it. Philip feels that Ramsay keeps him trapped in a kind of stasis—a pond or a tank in which they keep swimming in circles without the ability to change. Philip can feel that change may perhaps be forcing itself into the system as the temperature slowly, imperceptibly rises. Eventually the heat and pressure will build until something changes to fundamentally alter the system—an escape valve is needed if both are to avoid being "boiled."

Ultimately Philip arrives at Dennison's door one morning to confess the murder. The authors do not directly depict the murder; instead, there is only the murderer's explanation of it. The murder, like the relationship between Philip and Ramsay, remains a subject of speculation for the reader, who has only the perpetrator's account. Dennison and Ryko both seem to readily accept the story with almost no surprise. When Philip nonchalantly offers Dennison a smoke from Kammerer's blood-stained cigarette pack, he promptly advises Philip to get a lawyer. All three characters seem rather blasé about the murder, but Dennison at least takes a practical approach to the crime, encouraging Philip to pursue an "honor slaying" defense by claiming that Ramsay tried to rape him.

Philip initially ignores Dennison's advice and, two hours later, calls Ryko, who acts as an enabler in keeping Philip stuck in homeostasis without engaging with the inevitable change that must disrupt the pattern of the young man's life. The duo does not go immediately to the police; instead they have some drinks, attend a screening of *Four Feathers* (1939), and visit the Modern Museum of Art. Dennison picks up the story in the final chapter to detail the subsequent events. Dennison explains that Philip's wealthy and influential uncle got him committed to an asylum instead of jail. The chapter spends little time discussing Philip, but hints of the future Burroughs emerge when he discusses his interaction with the police: "The cops weren't too pleased about the way I knew about the murder and didn't rush to the nearest phone like a decent citizen who are all supposed to be stool pigeons according to the official ruling" (181). Apparent in this sentence is Burroughs's lifelong distrust for authority, particularly police officers, as well as his adherence to the Johnson code, a sort of thieves' code that transcends societal morality. A core belief of the Johnson code would be "You never rat." This last chapter gestures toward Burroughs's later work while also providing a kind of eulogy for the first phase of the Beat Generation that included only four members: Lucien Carr, Allen Ginsberg, William S. Burroughs, and Jack Kerouac. It was a period of innocent experimentation and intellectual curiosity that culminated in a murder, and death continued to haunt Burroughs and his oeuvre.

The Cellular Metamorphosis of Desire: Programming the Body in *Junky*

In his introduction to *Junky: The Definitive Text of Junk* (1953; "50th Anniversary Definitive Edition" 2003), Oliver Harris explained the permutations that the title of Burroughs's first published novel underwent. Burroughs's original title was simply "Junk," but the publishers wanted to make sure that the novel did not read as a pronarcotic text. Hence by the time it was published, the title was changed to *Junkie: Confessions of an Unredeemed Drug Addict* and was originally published as an Ace Double Edition together with Maurice Helbrant's novel *Narcotic Agent* (1941) to ensure that it was not seen as encouraging drug use. Subsequent editions of the novel altered the spelling to "*Junky*" instead of "*Junkie.*" *Junky* remains the most hard-boiled of Burroughs's novels with its use of street slang, its terse and edgy tone, and its depiction of drug addicts, hustlers, and criminals. By focusing on addiction, *Junky* deepens Burroughs's exploration of desire that began in *And the Hippos Were Boiled in Their Tanks,* and it adds the themes of control and metamorphosis, which become central to Burroughs's subsequent works. In fact Burroughs depicts drugs as an agent for reprogramming the human body in a truly posthuman way that is more minimalist and subtle in *Junkie* but that, nonetheless, presages the more radical works to come.

Junky was not the first work of literature to deal with opiate addiction. The literary tradition of recounting addiction stories stretches back to British Romantic author Thomas de Quincey's *Confessions of an English Opium-Eater* (1821) and includes French surrealist Jean Cocteau's *Opium: The Diary of His Cure* (1930). Other works fictionally depicted opium use: the notorious Aleister Crowley's *The Diary of a Drug Fiend* (1922) drew on his experiences with drug usage but in a completely fictional context, and Nelson Algren's *The Man with the Golden Arm* (1949) derived its content from Algren's experiences in post–World War II Chicago. Of all these works, Algren's *The Man with the Golden Arm* comes closest to Burroughs's novel because it also exhibits a hard-boiled aesthetic; yet Algren's novel proves more naturalistic as the reader watches the character crushed into dust by his environment and circumstances. Burroughs's works have a slight naturalistic tinge to them with their investigation of how various forces control the subject; however, they deviate wildly from naturalism with Burroughs's insistence that humanity can break free from such control. Of course these more philosophical points are presaged only in the vaguest of ways in *Junky.* The novel begins to delve into the relationship between desire and control, but it is not Eros (the erotic drive) that is on display in *Junky*—it is the dark side of desire, Thanatos (the death drive). But the novel is about more than just the desire for oblivion because it also explores the way junk reprograms the body according to the junkie's need and ability to satiate that need. Therefore *Junky* becomes a novel about the tripartite relationship between desire, the body, and control.

Many critics treat *Junky* as though it were a Kerouac novel, pointing out how the novel parallels Burroughs's life and discussing what it reveals about the literary icon. The novel does draw from Burroughs's first experiments with morphine in post–World War II New York City; his stint at Narcotics Hospital in Lexington, Kentucky; and his moves to New Orleans, Texas, and Mexico.

But focusing on the biographical can obscure Burroughs's already complex theoretical ideas. As he does in many of his works, Burroughs draws on his training as an anthropologist, and the novel is presented as a kind of report on the hipster underground—he even provides a glossary of hipster language. *Junky* includes fictional representations of many important people from Burroughs's life: Bill Gains, Herbert Huncke, Kells Elvins, and others. However, the novel never mentions the most traumatic event of Burroughs's time in Mexico—the accidental shooting of his wife. Instead the novel focuses on the various "habits" (addicted phases) that Burroughs developed with morphine, heroin, and other forms of "junk"; his attempts at rehabilitation; his forays into drug dealing; and his interactions with the junkies, hustlers, con men, and other denizens of the underworld that the narrator inhabits. The novel provides some hints about Burroughs's homosexuality, but they are never fully addressed, and his wife shows up only briefly. In actuality the reader would assume that Lee is a bachelor until the wife makes a sudden appearance. Burroughs proves uninterested in sexuality in this novel—Burroughs always claimed that junkies have no interest in sex. Instead *Junky* focuses on the development of Burroughs's theory of junk (his "pseudo-science" to use Jennie Skerl's term) and its ability to transform the body.

Junky concerns a man named William Lee (a pseudonym that Burroughs appropriated from his mother's maiden name and that he reused in subsequent works) who progresses from a dabbler in underworld dealings, such as selling stolen goods, to becoming a full-blown addict who thieves and connives to support his habit. The novel does not feature a plot progression in the ordinary sense; instead it is an episodic narrative, a structure much used in the picaresque tradition in which Burroughs participated. As Allen Hibbard explained, Burroughs's novels "are arranged rather than plotted. They do not operate according to the logic of conventional narratives" (19).[1] While the shady characters and criminal adventures keep *Junky* moving, it is the depiction of junk and addiction that proves most provocative in the novel.

Junky portrays "junk" as a substance that causes a metamorphosis in the human body, that pushes the human into a posthuman state reprogrammed by drugs. The novel's first instance of this occurs when Lee tries to help a friend move a tommy gun and a box of morphine syrettes (a dose of morphine contained in a disposable injector). A contact of his, Jack, provides the first image of the junkie body: "He had a clean-cut, healthy country face, but there was something curiously diseased about him. He was subject to sudden fluctuations in weight. . . . His face was lined with suffering in which his eyes did not participate. It was a suffering of his cells alone. He himself—the conscious ego that looked out of the glazed, alert-calm hoodlum eyes—would have nothing to do with this suffering of his rejected other self, a suffering of the nervous system, of flesh and viscera and cells" (3). In this passage Burroughs began developing his theory of junk cells, an idea that recurred throughout his early fiction, essays, and interviews. Junk has reprogrammed Jack's body to function like a biological computer. While not correct according to biological principles, Burroughs's view of the human body does jive with those of cybernetics and posthuman theory.

Lee continues discussing the junkie's bodily metamorphosis as he recounts his first habit. For starters he describes how junkies no longer crave social interaction or alcohol. He hypothesizes that "the body that has a quantity of junk in its cell will not absorb alcohol," leading to sickness instead of inebriation (18). Junk has reprogrammed the user's internal organs, and it also instigates changes in the largest organ of all—the human skin: "I also stopped bathing. When you are on junk, the feel of the water on the skin is unpleasant" (18). These symptoms appear so slowly that the junkie remains unaware that he has developed a habit until it has already possessed him: "All of a sudden, the addict looks in the mirror and does not recognize himself. The actual changes are difficult to specify, and they do not show up in the mirror. The addict himself has a special blind spot as far as the progress of his habit is concerned" (18–19). Behavior also begins to alter around the ritualistic practices of junk usage: "As a habit takes hold, other interests lose importance to the user. Life telescopes down to junk, one fix and looking forward to the next. . . . He does not realize that he is just going through the motions in his non-junk activities. It is not until his supply is cut off that he realizes what junk means to me" (19). Junk reprograms not just the human body but also the person's perception, identity, and behavior as well. Lee posits that this occurs because junk cells have replaced the healthy cells of the subject's body. In order to break a habit, junk cells must be starved of their sustenance, leading to "the death of junk-dependent cells and their replacement with cells that do not need junk" (19).

The novel proceeds to chronicle Lee's first experience of withdrawal, his attempts to get "scripts" from doctors, and his arrest (and mugging) by the police. Bailed out by his wife, who appears almost as an absence in the text since her character never receives a name or any characterization, Lee endures sickness and depression until he has "kicked" his habit. Soon Lee develops a heroin habit that requires him to resort to petty theft. Together with a coaddict named Roy, he starts "working the hole," which involves riding the subway and looking for "flops" (unconscious drunk men) to rob (28). From petty pickpocketing Lee soon progresses to becoming a dealer. Finally, with the pigeons squealing and the cops closing in, Lee retreats from the city and attempts a reduction cure on his own. Junk sick, Lee finally takes a train to Lexington to undergo the cure at the Narcotics Farm. After his cure Lee leaves Lexington for Texas and then New Orleans. The plot of the novel tends to repeat itself as Lee kicks a habit, begins using again, resorts to crime to support it, and eventually moves to another city, ultimately ending up in Mexico. The plot does not so much progress toward a climax as it spins new stories and characters in different turns of the addict's cycle; however what does build is the depiction of Lee's need for junk and his theory of junk's impact on the body.

In his 1965 *Paris Review* interview, Burroughs tried to succinctly explain his theory of junk and addiction:

> As I see it, what has been damaged in pain is, of course, the image, and morphine must in some sense replace this. We know it blankets the cells and that addicts are practically immune to certain viruses, to influenza and respiratory complaints. This is simple, because the influenza virus has to make a hole in the cell receptors. When those are covered, as they are in morphine addiction, the virus can't get in. As soon as morphine is withdrawn, addicts will immediately come down with colds and often with influenza. (Plimpton 8)

Burroughs's theory blends facts with pseudoscience because opiate addiction actually decimates the immune system, but this depiction of junk's effect on cellular structure becomes part of the overarching Burroughs mythos as does the idea that junkies become immune to viruses. When the junk gets withdrawn, the body revolts because its reprogrammed state has trouble resetting to its original cellular code. As Burroughs depicted the with the character Doolie, "the envelope of personality was gone, dissolved by his junk-hungry cells. Viscera and cells galvanized into a loathsome insect-like activity, seemed on the point of breaking through the surface. His face was blurred, unrecognizable, at the same time shrunken and tumescent" (48). In this passage junk and its withdrawal deform the identity of the addict as well as the body—the devolution into insect (or other bug) form will become a theme throughout Burroughs's fiction because the insect, centipede, or other bug has no significant brain activity. Instinct drives and controls it; similarly the junkie's identity and desire have been reduced to a pure instinct—to ingest junk. After he moves to New Orleans, Lee discovers the harsh drug laws of Louisiana, which remains infamous for its harshness toward users: "The state legislators drew up a law making it a crime to be an addict. They did not specify where or when or what they meant by drug addict" (66). Louisiana constitutes a space that has criminalized a certain form of identity similar to the way in which sodomy laws, which are also still on the books in Louisiana and many other states, strove to make homosexuality a punishable crime. The junkie has been labeled as what

Julia Kristeva would term the "abject," an individual not granted subjectivity by the forces of power.

Against the seemingly authoritarian backdrop of the United States, where identities such as addict and homosexual are criminal, Lee finally flees for the promise of freedom offered by Mexico. Unfortunately in Mexico City he discovers that pushing junk is impossible because Lupita controls the entire distribution network and has connections with the police that eliminate any potential rivals. Upon arrival Lee had kicked his junk habit, but as he states, "The mark of junk is indelible" (96). Once an individual has developed a junk habit, he remains recognizable despite kicking. Furthermore he remains only a few days away from developing a new habit: "An addict may be ten years off the junk, but he can get a new habit in less than a week" (97). Again Lee hypothesizes that this results from a biological mutation initiated by junk: "the use of junk causes permanent cellular alteration. Once a junkie, always a junkie. You can stop using junk, but you are never off after the first habit" (98). Lee eventually kicks his junk habit once again, only to become an alcoholic in its place. His alcoholism proves so severe that he develops borderline uremic poisoning, and the doctor suggests he return to junk instead of killing himself with alcohol.

Lee keeps tabs on the progression of drug laws in the United States, particularly the passage of the Harrison Narcotics Tax Act. First passed in 1914, the act dealt only with the regulation of opiates and coca derivates (cocaine, and the like), but subsequent related drug laws led to other drugs being made illegal. The Single Convention on Narcotic Drugs in 1961 banned the sale, possession, or usage of illegal drugs. These laws led directly to the criminalization of drug users and the birth of a black-market drug trade. Lee reads about drug users experimenting with peyote, the product of a certain cactus, because it was not labeled as illegal and grew naturally. Lee tries peyote but finds that it only makes him sick. The novel ends with Lee's kicking junk one last time, and, as he explains, "Like a man who has been away a long time, you see things different when you return from junk" (127). In this state Lee stumbles on the legends surrounding a South American drug known as yage, which can supposedly endow the user with telepathic abilities. Instead of highs that make the users internalize or retreat into their own consciousness, Lee believes that yage might be "the uncut kick that opens out instead of narrowing down like junk" (128). The novel ends with the line that "yage may be the final fix" (128). Ultimately junk has not fulfilled Lee's underlying desire for evolution, for tapping into unmapped areas of the brain, so he believes that other drugs might serve as the key to opening new posthuman abilities. Thus the novel ends with a new desire, a desire to reach outward and connect with others.

My Existential Hole Needs Filling: The Desire for Posthuman Intimacy in *Queer*

In many ways *Queer* constitutes nothing more than a tale of unrequited love, but the lover's ploys to capture his beloved's heart have more in common with those of Humbert Humbert in Vladimir Nabokov's *Lolita* (1955) than they do with those found in Dante's *La Vita Nuova* (1295) or Goethe's *The Sorrows of Young Werther* (1779). The novel depicts a desire from Burroughs's own life, a desire for an intimacy that extends beyond mere penetration and ejaculation and into the realm of two selves literally becoming one, a love that he believes will make them whole. Like Humbert Burroughs manipulates his love into sexual acts and seeks to control him in various ways. Thus while *Junky* depicted the dark side of desire—Thanatos—*Queer* shifts the focus to Eros but not without abandoning Burroughs's interest in the intertwined nature of desire and control. *Queer* reads like a sequel to *Junky* because it picks up with a fictionalized depiction of his time in Mexico and his first quests for yage. But yage is only a peripheral desire in the novel because Allerton represents the true treasure that Burroughs seeks.

Burroughs wrote *Queer* between 1951 and 1953, but its subject matter was deemed taboo at the time, so it remained unpublished until 1985. Most criticism has focused on the introduction that Burroughs penned for the novel because it is the first time that he discussed the accidental shooting of his common-law wife—Joan Vollmer. While the introduction proves fascinating from a biographical perspective and does highlight Joan's death as the one major piece of Burroughs's life missing from this early trilogy, the novel (or novella one might properly call it owing to its brevity) proves interesting for more important reasons: it shows Burroughs first developing his writing of routines, and it further develops a posthuman view of the human body as an object susceptible to control and mutation via the force of desire.

With *Queer* Burroughs shifted from a first-person narrator to a third-person limited omniscient one that focuses on the psyche and experiences of William Lee. The novel opens appropriately with a scene of rejection. Lee is trying to establish a sexual relationship with a young man named Carl: "What Lee looked for in any relationship was the feel of contact. He felt some contact with Carl" (2). Despite Carl's not being gay, Lee persists in the hope that he might "be obliging," but Carl eventually bids him a courteous farewell and leaves with his family for Uruguay. Left in a state of profound depression and desirous of a connection, Lee focuses on Eugene Allerton. Unfortunately Lee's first effort to connect culminates with his mumbling and being "froze[n] in front of a restaurant like a bird dog" (14). All initial attempts to woo Allerton fail miserably: "Lee tried to achieve a greeting at once friendly and casual, designed to show interesting without pushing a short acquaintance. The result was ghastly" (15). This performance in many ways foreshadows Lee's attempts at intimacy throughout the novel as he seeks sex and companionship from young men who are incapable of giving him both.

After several more abortive attempts at an introduction, Lee finally meets up with a drunk Allerton in the Ship Ahoy, one of several bars he frequents. In his inebriated state, Allerton reveals a carefree, loquacious persona that revels in telling stories. This development heightens Lee's desire to an almost intolerable level:

> An imaginary hand projected with such force it seemed Allerton must feel the touch of ectoplasmic fingers caressing his ear, phantom thumbs smoothing his eyebrows, pushing hair back from his face. Now Lee's hands were running down over the ribs, the stomach. Lee felt the aching pain of desire in his lungs. His mouth was a little open, showing his teeth in the half snarl of a baffled animal. He licked his lips. Lee did not enjoy frustration. The limitations of his desires were like the bars of a cage, like a chain and collar, something he had learned as an animal learns, through the days and years of experiencing the snub of the chain, the unyielding bars. (23)

In *Queer* Lee experiences lack in its purest form: beginning with the lack of heroin and moving into the lack of sex and culminating in his lack of a reciprocated love.

The notion of lack has been defined in two related yet distinct fashions in both the existential philosophy of Levinas and Sartre and the psychoanalysis of Jacques Lacan. In existentialism the individual is faced with the lack of meaning in the universe, a lack of essence. To lead a purposeful life, the individual must create his own essence; that is, his own sense of identity and ethics. Jacques Lacan's concept of lack is related to his theory of signifiers and their relationship to the subject, concepts that will prove important to Burroughs's later writings as well. Lee's character had formerly achieved sublimation via junk—junk was the master signifier that made sense of his existence. Junk, as Lee explains in both *Junky* and at the beginning of *Queer,* eliminates the user's sex drive. Hence when the substitute object of junk gets taken away, the old lack of sexual satisfaction rears its head and begins to spur Lee's desire for young men. Sexual desire returns as "naked lust," leaving him in a state like a mad dog chomping at the bit. When Lee meets Allerton in a drunken state, Allerton takes a liking to his conversational abilities, and the two begin meeting every day at the same bar where Lee regales Allerton with his routines, a storytelling method that Burroughs first developed in his letters to Allen Ginsberg and would refine even further in *Naked Lunch*. The novel breaks briefly with its limited omniscient narrator to provide the reader with a glimpse into Allerton's mind. In one of these moments, the narrator reveals that Allerton feels smothered and confused by Lee from the beginning: "But Allerton felt at times oppressed by Lee, as though Lee's presence shut off everything else. He thought he was seeing too much of Lee. Allerton disliked commitments and had never been in love or had a close friend. He was forced to ask himself 'What does he want from me?' It did not occur to him that Lee was queer, as he associated queerness with at least some degree of overt effeminacy" (24–25). Allerton assumes that he just wants an audience for his routines, and his ideas of homosexuality remain trapped in the stereotypes of femininity generally associated with gay men. Thus Allerton allows their friendship to develop because he believes that Lee has nothing more than Platonic intentions.

The first routine that Lee performs for Allerton constitutes an almost direct come-on: "The Texas Oilman" routine depicts a "redneck" con man. The story culminates in a discussion of "dry holes," oil wells that never produce; as the oilman says, "Some holes got lubrication and some is dry as a whore's cunt on Sunday Morning" (30). The routine gives Lee an opportunity for comedy as he performs the backwoods accents and expressions while also alluding to anal sex: he "figured it was time to let Allerton know what the score was. Such a thing as playing it too cool" (30). After that night Allerton and Lee attend a screening of Jean Cocteau's surrealist masterpiece *Orpheus* (1950). Lee feels an almost unbearable desire to become one with Allerton: "Lee could feel his body pull toward Allerton, an amoeboid protoplasmic projection, straining with a blind worm of hunger to enter the other's body, to breathe with his lungs, see with his eyes, learn the feel of his viscera and genitals" (33). While this may seem like a body horror metaphor for the lover's desire to join with his lover—to become one—Burroughs meant it much more literally. It is an idea that Burroughs called "schlupping": the physical joining of two people into one physical being or even the assimilation of one lover by the other.

Lee has developed a form of desire that could be characterized as posthuman because it breaks down the walls of the both the body and the subject's identity. However, getting Allerton to engage in such a relationship when he already despises the slightest hint of commitment proves problematic for Lee. Allerton finally discovers Lee's sexual preferences from a shared friend. In typical style Lee responds with a routine: "A curse . . . been in our family for generations. The Lees have always been perverts. I shall never forget the unspeakable horror that froze the lymph in my glands . . . when the baneful word seared my reeling brain: *homosexual*. I was a homosexual" (35). Lee continues to regale Allerton with the stereotypes that populated his young mind regarding gay men—his image of homosexuality includes only the "drag queens" that he had witnessed walking the streets. Drag queens are, of course, not necessarily gay, but young Lee's mind had only received the social stigmas that are often blanketly applied to all non-cisgender people even to this day. Ironically it is a drag queen named "Bobo" who first taught Lee to accept his sexuality: she "taught me that I had a duty to live and to bear my burden proudly for all to see, to conquer prejudice and ignorance and hate with knowledge and sincerity and love" (35–36). The routine ends—like most Burroughs routines—with grotesque black humor: Bobo's "falling piles blew out of the car and wrapped around the real wheel. He was completely gutted, leaving an empty shell sitting there on the giraffe-skin upholstery" (36). Despite this grotesque finale, Lee finishes the story with a tender epilogue. After Bobo's death, Lee begins to experience loneliness and despair, but Bobo's positivity returns to him: "No one is ever really alone. You are part of everything alive" (36). This passage sounds like the kind of comforting platitude one resorts to in the face of death; however it also connects to Lee's desire to schlupp. For whatever reason this routine works on Allerton, who agrees to join Lee for brandy back at his place. Although Allerton readily succumbs to Lee's seduction, Lee does notice "a curious detachment, the impersonal calm of an animal or a child" (40). Afterward Lee offers to pay to get Allerton's phone out of hock at a pawn shop, attempting to further cement their relationship by causing Allerton to depend on him financially.

After a complacent period of seeing Allerton, Lee eventually gets rejected in a way that sends him spiraling back into desperate depression: "In any relation of love or friendship, Lee attempted to establish contact on the nonverbal level of intuition, a silent exchange of thought and feeling. Now Allerton had abruptly shut off contact, and Lee felt a physical pain, as though a part of himself tentatively stretched out toward the other had been severed, and he was looking at the bleeding stump in shock and disbelief" (50). After reflecting on the incident and his situation with Allerton, Lee decides that "Allerton was not queer enough to make a reciprocal relation possible" (52). Here Lee depicts queerness as a spectrum, an idea that has much in common with contemporary gender and queer theory, particularly since Judith Butler. Despondent Lee begins to ponder methods of rekindling his relationship with Allerton even if the adoration remains one-sided.

Lee became fascinated with a South American drug called yage that could supposedly induce telepathy. In the hopes of learning to expand human consciousness, Lee plans an expedition to South America, which he believes might be the perfect bait to entice Allerton back into his affections. Wary of losing his independence, Allerton initially remains hesitant, but Lee offers him a deal:

"So who's going to cut in on your independence? You can lay all the women in South America if you want to. All I ask is be nice to Papa, say twice a week. That isn't excessive, is it? Besides, I will buy you a round-trip ticket so you can leave at your discretion" (62). Here Lee rather creepily turns Allerton into a kind of prostitute while simultaneously putting himself in the role of pimp-father-lover.

Lee sets their destination as Bogotá, Colombia, where a scientist has supposedly isolated the telaphine (the telepathy inducing chemical or compound) in yage. The pair embark on their expedition, but Allerton begins to chaff against Lee's desires before they even reach Panama City. Eventually the two fly to Quito, Ecuador's capital, where Lee becomes junk sick. The junk sickness causes the return of Lee's libido: "I'm a little junk sick, you know, and that makes me sooo sexy. The neighbors could witness some innaresting sights" (77). Allerton quickly puts a stop to Lee's inept attempt at seduction by citing "breach of contract" since Allerton had already met his "twice a week" quota. Here Lee hits the wall of their contractual relationship, and he explains the appeal of yage: "'Think of it; thought control. Take anyone apart and rebuild to your taste.' . . . He looked at Allerton and licked his lips. 'You'd be so much *nicer* after a few alterations. You're nice now, of course, but you do have those irritating little peculiarities. I mean you won't do exactly what I want you to do all the time'" (80). Here Lee comes to desire the very control that Burroughs so adamantly abhors and challenges throughout most of his writings.

Lee continues to discuss his desire for control over Allerton as the conversation shifts to "automatic obedience," a state associated with certain schizophrenics. The behavior manifests itself in catatonic states but is not necessarily present in all schizophrenics. Lee, then, extrapolates the condition from the individual to the social level: "Whatever I say, whatever anyone says, you must do. Get the picture? A pretty picture isn't it? so long as you are the one giving the orders that are automatically obeyed. Automatic obedience, synthetic schizophrenia, mass-produced to order. That is the Russian dream, and America is not far behind. The bureaucrats of both countries want the same thing: Control. The super-ego, the controlling agency, gone cancerous and berserk" (81).

Lee begins to ponder the possibility of a society in which "there is no limit," and "he felt a killing hate for the stupid, ordinary, disapproving people who kept him from doing what he wanted to do" (86–87). Lee's thoughts and conversations begin to push into disturbing, Sadean space. Eventually Lee expresses his uninhibited fantasies to Allerton, particularly his desire to physically merge with a lover: "'Wouldn't it be booful if we could just run together into one gweat big blob,' he said in baby talk. 'Am I giving you the horrors?'" (89). Allerton admits his discomfort but makes passionate love to Lee anyway;

however, the episode foreshadows the decline of their contracted relationship. Allerton voyages on with Lee through the Andes and to the town of Puyo, Ecuador, where Lee first begins asking around for yage. The locals prove unwilling to provide it to strangers, but Lee gets a lead on a botanist experimenting with the drug in the jungle nearby. Cotter, the botanist, explains that Lee would need to meet a *brujo* (a wizard or shaman-like figure). The main narrative of the novel, which was divided into chapters, ends abruptly here. The novel's final section, an epilogue entitled "Two Years Later: Mexico City Return," shifts from third-person to first-person narration. Still obsessed with Allerton, Lee returns to Panama and Mexico City in hopes of finding him. Lee sadly ponders, "He must have gotten my letters. Why didn't he answer? Why?" (113) Burroughs switches to first person in this final section to allow Lee to personally express his internal pain and desire. The novel opens with Lee seeking a connection, and it comes full circle with his still trying to find someone to fill the lack that he experiences so profoundly.

The Evolutionary Impulse: The Search for Higher Consciousness in *The Yage Letters*

Many readers and critics often try to force *The Yage Letters* into an autobiographical trilogy with *Junky* and *Queer* because it continues the confessional form and the narrative aspects of his two previous works. The book remains hard to even classify because it constitutes a hybrid text: it is not a novel but also not a simple collection of letters. *The Yage Letters* resembles other books of inner exploration and the alteration of consciousness from the same period: Aldous Huxley's *The Doors of Perception* (1956) and *Heaven and Hell* (1956) or Carlos Castaneda's *The Teachings of Don Juan: A Yaqui Way of Knowledge* (1968). Ken Russell's later film *Altered States* (1980) features scientists experimenting with the combination of hallucinogenic drugs and sensory-deprivation tanks. This research leads the protagonist on a Castaneda-style trip to Mexico where he also imbibes yage, which eventually allows him to access atavistic forms of consciousness. While comparisons can prove helpful, *The Yage Letters* ultimately avoids classification as it plays out as a quest narrative on two different levels: the physical quest through South America and the spiritual and intellectual quest to achieve higher states of consciousness and awareness.

The novel consists of three sections: "In Search of Yage" (the bulk of the work), "Seven Years Later," and "Epilogue." Burroughs shares authorial credit with Allen Ginsberg on every edition of *The Yage Letters,* but Ginsberg's contributions make up a minimal (if not unnecessary) section of the novel in the latter two sections, which were not a part of the original *The Yage Letters* manuscript. Yage (or ayahuasca) is a brew made from the *Banisteriopsis caapi* vine, which is used in various spiritual ceremonies among certain indigenous peoples in South America.[2] Furthermore the novel is not actually a collection of letters. Burroughs wrote to Allen Ginsberg constantly throughout the 1950s, but, as Oliver Harris pointed out in his edition of *The Yage Letters,* Burroughs took the travelogue he was writing of his trip and "fabricated its epistolary appearance by adding material such as the letter's formal tops and tails, by changing the tense to create an improvised sense of reporting live, and by cutting out tell-tale lines" (xxxiii). Harris further explained that Burroughs did cull some material from actual letters but then mixed it with his journal entries or even added new material (xxxiii). Therefore *The Yage Letters* proves more autobiographical than *Junky* or *Queer,* but the book should not be read in the same manner as Burroughs's collections of letters or journals. For a more unadulterated look at Burroughs's inner thoughts and experiences, the reader should look to *Everything Lost: The Latin American Notebooks of William S. Burroughs* (written 1953; published 1992), a beautiful edition, edited by Oliver Harris, that provides facsimiles of Burroughs's own handwritten notebook pages while also providing the reader with a fair copy and a critical apparatus.

The Yage Letters opens with a letter from Panama, where Bill (as he styles himself in most of the letters) has stopped off to have his "piles out"—a hemorrhoidectomy (3). Once again Bill is striving to give up junk while his friend Bill Gains argues that "once a junkie always a junkie" (3). Like *Queer*, *The Yage Letters* opens with junk sickness and lack, which drive the narrator to find some new means of fulfilling his lack. The second letter finds Bill in Bogotá on the quest for yage, which may constitute a means of jumpstarting the evolution of the human mind. He meets a Dr. Schindler, who suggests a trip to the Putumayo region as "the most readily accessible" but warns that the telepathy legends are all "imagination" (9). Disregarding this Bill travels through Colombia and discovers the major mechanisms of control that operate in the region: the Policía Nacional and the Catholic Church. Bill claims that "in Bogota[3] more than any other city I have seen in Latin America you feel the dead weight of Spain somber and oppressive. Everything official bears the label Made in Spain" (10). Of course Colombia had been free of Spanish rule since 1819, and Spain, at the time, was deep into the fascist regime of Francisco Franco. Still the neocolonial atmosphere persists with a ruling body that in no way represents most of its population.

Approaching Interzone—the Composite City

"Interzone" was the working title for *Naked Lunch,* but the collection features not only sections that were cut from *Naked Lunch* but also earlier writings that led to *Naked Lunch*. Aside from his juvenilia discussed in the introduction,

Burroughs's first significant writing was a collaboration with lifelong friend Kells Elvins entitled "Twilight's Last Gleaming," a text that would get recycled in various ways throughout Burroughs's later writings and that first introduced his most iconic character—Dr. Benway. The story concerns an explosion on and the subsequent sinking of a ship filled with mostly upper-class passengers as well as Dr. Benway who (for whatever reason) is simultaneously performing surgery on the ship. The story recalls the sinking of the *Titanic*, particularly the fact that the band keeps playing as the ship sinks to pacify the passengers. However, in Burroughs's version this role is filled by a "Negro orchestra, high on marijuana," who prove less valiant because they flee the scene while a jukebox plays "The Star-Spangled Banner." Single lyrics from the anthem interject themselves at the end of paragraphs to divide up the different scenes of chaos aboard the sinking ship. Burroughs and Elvins use the anthem ironically to undermine its alleged power. The anthem, of course, constitutes part of the essential American mythology: Francis Scott Key witnessed the British naval attack on Fort McHenry, saw the American flag still flying in the morning, and wrote a poem about the ability of the American spirit to endure no matter what the odds. The story ultimately demonstrates how little a flag means to people as they drown in the ocean; furthermore those who survive are not necessarily the innocent. As the unsuspecting passengers attempt to board the lifeboats, Dr. Benway abandons surgery in favor of his own safety. During the surgery Benway was trying to extract the appendix on the wrong side and smoking while making an incision. After the explosion rocks the boat, he snatches all the cocaine and morphine into his doctor's bag. Like a coward he boards a lifeboat full of women and children, stating "Are you all right? . . . I'm the doctor" (10). The doctor's incompetence coupled with his cowardice directly parody the national anthem that keeps playing. Unfortunately there is no flag flying at the end—the ship sinks, and the reprehensible (albeit hilarious) Dr. Benway remains one of the survivors, proving that the American ideal constitutes nothing more than hollow propaganda.

"The Finger" is a rather unremarkable early story that provides a fictional recreation of the time that Burroughs chopped off the top joint of his finger to impress a man. In the story this character gets transformed into a female character à la Proust and Albertine in *In Search of Lost Time*. The story culminates in his being committed to the Bellevue psychiatric ward. Burroughs's pity for the severed joint recalls the woman's pity for the severed finger at the end of "Twilight's Last Gleaming." This represented just one of many instances of unrequited love that he would endure throughout his life. As James Grauerholz explained in his introduction, the story "Driving Lesson" provides a fictional recounting of an automobile accident that he experienced in his hometown of

St. Louis while visiting his friend Jack Anderson (xv–vi). These stories fit with the aesthetic of *Junky* and other confessional Beat literature, but they provide little of interest except as artifacts of Burroughs's early attempts at narrative.

One of Burroughs's more poignant works, "The Junky's Christmas" returns to the world of *Junky* with the reappearance of 103rd Street and Pantopon Rose. In the end the story recalls such Christmas stories of self-sacrifice as O. Henry's "The Gift of the Magi," except it has been filtered through the lens of the squalor, pain, and addiction of the urban space in which the main character, Danny the Car Wiper, dwells. Freshly out of prison on Christmas, a junk-sick Danny spends the day trying to score as he visits friends and dealers without any luck. Finally Danny visits a "croaker" (doctor) at his home and begs for a morphine prescription to treat the pain of facial neuralgia (a contrived condition). The doctor eventually gives him a single pill, and, after collecting the necessary paraphernalia, he checks into a dirt-cheap hotel to shoot up. After cooking up and preparing his injection, Danny begins to hear groans of pain through the thin walls. Checking next door he finds a man in agony from his kidney stones (a disease that Danny had often faked), and he cannot receive medical care because the hospital staff and doctors assume he is just a junkie looking to score because of his location. In the ultimate sacrifice, Danny administers the injection to the man, who soon falls asleep peacefully. As Danny begins to clean up the evidence on the off chance that the room gets "tossed" (investigated by police), he has a strange experience: "Suddenly a warm flood pulsed through his veins and broke his head like a thousand golden speedballs. *For Christ's sake,* Danny thought. *I must have scored for the immaculate fix!*" (31).[4] The term *immaculate*, of course, recalls the impregnation of Mary, and Danny believes some divine force has rewarded his good deed: "The vegetable serenity of junk settled in his tissues. His face went slack and peaceful, and his head fell forward. Danny the Car Wiper was on the nod" (31). Danny's act of selflessness finally allows him to experience the peace promised by the Christmas season. The story can ultimately be interpreted in two ways: (1) as an ironic satire of sappy Christmas stories or (2) as an authentic attempt to bring a gritty, hard-boiled aesthetic to saccharine Christmas stories such as O. Henry's "Gift of the Magi." While the story can be read with Burroughs's biting wit, it also seems plausible that he intends for it to be read as an ethical tale because Danny upholds the Johnson code, the form of ethics that Burroughs believes in, by helping his neighbor. Burroughs will continue to develop his conceptualization of the Johnson code throughout the rest of his works.

The remainder of the stories in *Interzone*'s first part are unremarkable except for the fact that they feature the straightforward style of *Junky* and *Queer*, but they shift the action to Tangier, where *Naked Lunch* will predominately take place. The stories do not require lengthy exposition; however, the reader can get a glimpse into how Burroughs might have depicted his life in Tangier if his work had not undergone the seismic shift of style that is *Naked Lunch*. *Interzone*'s second section, entitled "Lee's Journals," continues the fictionalized account of his life, but it features two important moments: (1) it mentions the death of Joan Vollmer, and (2) it discusses the darkness of Burroughs's childhood that he felt persisted through events such as Joan's death. The discussion of her death is brief and does not provide detail, but it is the most she appears in Burroughs's early writings except for her brief cameo in *Junky*. Aside from interviews Burroughs would not mention her again in his own writings until his introduction to *Queer*. Furthermore the section connects Joan's death to the trauma of Burroughs's childhood, which he tried to remember and understand throughout his life. Taken together with Burroughs's first four novels, *Interzone* fills in many gaps that depict his process of evolving from competent novelist to experimental icon.

CHAPTER 3

The End of Their Forks

The Microphysics of Power in *Naked Lunch*

While early routines from his letters, *Queer,* and *The Yage Letters* presage the radical mutation that Burroughs's work would undergo, *Naked Lunch* constitutes the sea change that not only established his own unique style but also fundamentally influenced so much literature and culture that came afterward with its blend of hard-boiled narrative, science fiction, graphic sex and violence, and surrealist extremes. This chapter resumes chapter 2's examination of the *Interzone* anthology by looking at the works that were excised from the final *Naked Lunch* manuscript, particularly "Word." Many critics have tried to force a coherent narrative on *Naked Lunch* about a junkie moving from one place to another until he arrives in a place called Interzone, which may or may not be a hallucination. Such critics read *Naked Lunch* from a modernist perspective—they read it as a stream-of-consciousness narrative and attempt to force a meaningful structure on its fragmented surface as if they were reading James Joyce's *Ulysses* (1922) or William Faulkner's *The Sound and the Fury* (1929). Many readers have attempted to connect the dots of the novel in a linear sense that chronicles a junkie's hallucinogenic flight from New York to the American South and finally to Tangier. In many ways such a reading renders the novel safe, trying to turn it into a rabbit hole or Oz-like experience in which reality prevails over fantasy, thus robbing the nonsensical of its power by forcing structure, coherence, and rationality on it. As Robin Lyndenberg argued, one cannot read *Naked Lunch* as allegory, satire, or didactic track; instead one must take it literally as Burroughs intended: "The literalness—mathematical, scientific, naturalistic, supernaturalistic—which pervades Burroughs' prose style is part of his campaign to free literature from morality and symbolic rhetoric, to seize for it the independence of the sciences" (13). *Naked Lunch* cannot be constrained by linear, chronological time—Burroughs would spend the rest of his literary career trying to find the means of escaping time. Instead the novel is episodic—as picaresque novels of the past had been—and "spill[s] off the page in all directions" (*Interzone* 135). However, certain overall themes can be discussed, for it constitutes the first time that Burroughs truly grappled with the question of control on levels that range from the individual to the social while exploring whether desire constitutes a means for revolution or just another site for control to manipulate.

Burroughs always maintained that *Naked Lunch* could be opened to any page and still make sense. *Naked Lunch* remains entirely episodic, leaving the reader to contemplate whether there is an overarching narrative (there is not), whether the episodes are linked thematically (yes, but it is still not that easy), and whether the novel ends up constituting anything more than drug-induced, violent, pornographic prose that ultimately has no purpose. This was the reading that many censorious individuals at the time espoused, but *Naked Lunch* proves to be so much more—it is a Sadean carnival of delights and horrors that bores into the core of human nature and the power structures that attempt to control it. Burroughs's universe is chaotic, but the forces of control try to force order on it. *Naked Lunch* remains primarily dystopian because it does not show a way out as do his later works—he leads a journey through both the abjects and the controllers to demonstrate how the control system attempts to tame the abject and render them subject to control.

Naked Novella: *Word* and Other *Naked Lunch* Precursors

The bulk of the stories in *Interzone* fall into the same aesthetic as *Junky* and *Queer,* but several of the later works in *Interzone* begin charting Burroughs's progression from writing confessional literature, like his Beat friends, into the realm of experimental literature, after which point he had more in common with the surrealists and avant-garde artists than with the Beat circle. Burroughs always grumbled about his being categorized as a Beat author despite his early position and influence within the group. The stories "Spare-Ass Annie" and "Ginsberg Notes" as well as the novella *Word* begin to develop the theme of body horror, the practice of routines, and the attack on language that came to fruition in *Naked Lunch*.

One of the later stories in "Lee's Journals," "Spare-Ass Annie" became somewhat famous as the title of one of Burroughs's albums. The story fits right alongside such *Naked Lunch* routines as the talking asshole. The story's unnamed town begins to provide sanctuary for those individuals that society has deemed abject, particularly those with "disgusting and disquieting deformities" (102).

Burroughs staged these abject individuals as the heroes, all of whom feature "deformities" of a sexual nature. There is Centipeder (centipede on top and human on bottom) who constantly makes sexual advances to anyone around, thus giving rise to his nickname that plays on the word "peter" (common slang for penis). Fish Cunt Sara, a "hermaphrodite" (or "intersexed," as it would be termed now) "claimed he was the best lay in town" (102). The titular character "Spare-Ass Annie" featured "an auxiliary asshole in the middle of her forehead, like a baneful bronze eye" (102). This secondary anus sits at the place of the sixth chakra, known as the third eye, often associated with telepathy and astral projection, practices that always fascinated Burroughs. The fact that the asshole is "auxiliary" implies that it is functional and that perhaps the excretion of physical matter is not enough. The mind also requires purging of the shit that has accumulated in it, the propaganda and techniques of power that have attempted to maintain control by preserving the binary between subject and abject based on bodily demarcations. Here the abject becomes the master, as these individuals form a society complete with "priests who carried out strange rites." Women who birthed "monstrosities" were prized because they "humilat[ed] the human race before the gods, in the hopes of diverting the anger of the gods" (103). Ultimately the society's search for freedom from control ends in merely instantiating a new system of control with their priests, their rites, and their gold stars.

"Ginsberg Notes" reads almost like Burroughs's journal that continues the story from the Mexican and South American setting of *Queer* and *The Yage Letters* into Burroughs's life in Tangier; however, it begins to demonstrate Burroughs's newly developed form of storytelling that he called the "routine," a story that blends realistic elements together with fantastic ones almost always with a dry, pitch-black sense of humor. Tangier starts to be depicted as "Interzone" in this story-journal, paving the way for its full-blown introduction in the long unpublished "Word." At one point Lee describes himself writing furiously and laughing out loud at the material he has produced: "These routines will reduce me to a cinder, like the Technician. And how can I ever write a 'novel'? The 'novel' is a dead form, rigid and arbitrary. I can't use it" (126). Burroughs had to shuffle off the mortal coil of the novel, a genre or structure that constrains and controls. He sought freedom from the chains that bound him in *Junky* and *Queer* and even in the somewhat experimental epistolary novel *The Yage Letters.*

The final sections of "Ginsberg Notes" provide a kind of prolegomenon to "Word," which lays out Burroughs's theoretical approach. "Word" provides only a glimpse of what is to come, but it opens with a strong methodological statement: "The word is divided into units which be all in one piece and should be so taken, but the pieces can be had in any order being tied up back and forth in and out fore and aft like an innaresting sex arrangement. The book spill off the page in all directions, kaleidoscope of vistas, medley of tunes and street noises, farts and riot yipes and the slamming steel shutters of commerce, screams of pain and pathos and screams plain pathetic" (135). The passage reads almost like a section of Joyce's *Ulysses,* particularly "Aeolus" and "Sirens," in which the perception of chaotic sounds invades Leopold Bloom's stream of consciousness. However, Burroughs's purpose is different than Joyce's—Joyce provided multiple underlying schematic ways of unifying the fragmented surface of the novel, the most famous of which is how the story parallels Homer's *Odyssey.* Any unity perceived in *Naked Lunch* is merely a product of the reader's own imagination. Even the kaleidoscope that Burroughs mentioned proves to be a poor metaphor because the kaleidoscope still features its fractal-like patterns that oscillate in and out as the viewer turns the tube.

Shortly after this opening, he announced the project that would continually obsess him throughout his life: the destruction of the word, the most basic of control mechanisms: "The word, gentle reader, will flay you down to the laughing bone and the author will do a striptease with his own intestines. Let it be. No holds barred" (136). Here Burroughs played on the word "striptease," which both conjures the general meaning of erotic disrobing while also recalling "flaying," the stripping of flesh as a form of torture. Via the word the reader is "stripped" with "ease," not just beneath the dermal layer but all the way down to the bone. Thus Burroughs has announced the power of the word, its power to control and organize a subject from the bones up. However, as Deleuze and Guattari would say, the bones (just like organs) constitute a form of structure even when the body has been stripped away. Burroughs planned to go further than the word, to smash the word and its power by demolishing the bones themselves, crushing them to dust to achieve what Deleuze and Guattari term a body without organs (and even without bones in this case), without any model of organization. Only when this destruction of organization is achieved can the subject (or the abject) consider real freedom: the demolishment and transcendence of the body to a higher form of evolution. Like Nietzsche, Burroughs proposed to philosophize (or write) with a hammer, to destroy all that had come before in favor of absolute becoming. For Deleuze and Guattari, the body without organs (or bones) represents such a space of free creation, of writing one's life free from the strictures placed on it by biology, society, morality, and so on. As Burroughs said, "The Author will spare his gentle readers nothing but strip himself brother naked. Description? I bugger it" (137). His words here presage how Deleuze describes his books on other philosophers: Spinoza, Leibniz, Hume, Kant, and Nietzsche. Deleuze claimed that he took a philosopher from behind (buggered or fucked in the ass) to produce a kind of monstrous offspring, an offspring born of anal intercourse. Burroughs sought to unleash a similar horde of monsters that would destroy language, society, and morality at their base, eating away, eviscerating, and raping all the structures that society holds so dear. "Word" serves as an appetizer to the heavy lunch at hand. At times it proceeds in a fashion even more radical than *Naked Lunch*—no chapters divide "Word"—it unfolds with one horror or perversion after the next, leaving the reader adrift in a sea of meaninglessness and "depravity" with no bearings to guide him- or herself home. Readers must simply take the ride and hope they emerge from the other side of this deep dive into absolute abjectness. If they do emerge, they will no doubt be changed.

"Devil doll stool pigeons": A Hard-Boiled Opening

However simple *Naked Lunch's* opening seems, the chapter represents just one in a collage of episodes that never quite fit together—there is no overarching picture that will emerge at the end, and sanity certainly will not prevail. The beginning might trick the reader, as it has many readers and critics, into believing that the novel has a linear narrative, but this desire for narrative ultimately stems from the readers' desire for the comfort of logic—humans themselves string together their lives and identities via narrative to create a stable version of themselves, a version that Nietzsche, Deleuze, and Burroughs completely disavow. The novel opens with perhaps the most hard-boiled line in Burroughs's body of work: "I can feel the heat closing in, feel them out there making their moves, setting up their devil doll stool pigeons, crooning over my spoon and dropper I throw away at Washington Square Station" (3). The novel again features the character of William Lee in the first chapter. "And Start West" immediately baptizes the reader back into the world of junkies and criminals from *Junky;* however, already in these early chapters Burroughs's writing proves more poetic. The prose bristles with a chaotic, electric energy that proves as constantly funny as it does disturbing. After Lee ditches the "narcotics dick" who was "trying to pass as a fag," the first in a long line of Burroughs characters who will misrepresent their gender or sexuality, Lee decides to "catnip" some "square" who is looking for "pod," meaning that he intends to swindle the naive young man by selling him catnip instead of marijuana (3–5).

Naked Lunch begins to slowly inject body horror into the mix as sci-fi and horror elements begin to seep into the hard-boiled narrative. The novel's genre, which will eventually become a meaningless term before its final section, begins to shift slowly with the story of Bradley the Buyer, someone "so anonymous, grey and spectral" that he "can walk up to a pusher and score direct" without the pusher "remember[ing] him afterwards" (14). Unfortunately the Buyer's deep cover operations take a toll on him as he begins undergoing bodily transformations. He develops the full symptomology of the junky, but his metamorphoses take the junky characteristics to new levels—perhaps the Buyer evolves into what the human would become on a long enough timeline if everyone was addicted to junk. He starts off with typical junky symptoms: his teeth fall out, he becomes impotent, he develops an inability to consume alcohol, and he then undergoes a radical metamorphosis: "The Buyer takes on an ominous grey-green color. Fact is his body is making its own junk or equivalent. The Buyer has a steady connection, A Man Within, you might say" (15). Despite his production of junk, the Buyer still experiences a "yen" that cannot be satiated by himself, so he seeks out a young junkie to whom he gives a paper. The young junkie always assumes that he requires sexual payment, but the Buyer just wants to rub against the youth while he gets high. After the encounter the boy later explains, "Most distasteful thing I ever stood still for. . . . Some way he makes himself all soft like a blob of jelly and surround me so nasty. Then he gets wet all over like with green slime. So I guess he came to some kind of awful climax" (15). Regardless of all the nastiness, the boy already has an appointment set up for the next day because "it's still an easy score" (15).

While it is already been seen how junk reprograms the user's body, *Naked Lunch* begins to delve into the symbiotic relationship between the two, each providing the other with a substance or service that he or she requires. With real junkies and buyers, the junkie exchanges money for drugs, money that the dealer often uses to maintain his own habit. However, this scene demonstrates how the symbiotic relationship can become skewed to one side as the dealer comes to overtake the Buyer's life, feeding off his life force. Soon one junkie proves insufficient, and he will bribe himself into prison cells full of junkies to feed—almost vampire-like—off multiple victims at once. Finally his habit becomes all-consuming—the Within can no longer provide enough junk to fix the Buyer. Ravenous and caught in a recursive loop where the ability to get high recedes in a *mise en abyme* fashion like repeating images in a series of mirrors, the Buyer's increasingly erratic behavior finally catches the attention of the higher-ups, and he is called in before the district supervisor, who rebukes him. The Buyer sucks on the supervisor's fingers and offers all kind of deviant favors in exchange for lenience. The supervisor finds this "distasteful" and orders the Buyer to leave. But the Buyer's body "begins to dip like a dowser's wand," homing in on its object of desire—here the human body has become a more essential necessity than water or even junk itself. In other words, the Buyer can no longer live by bread alone—he must consume life: his relationship with other human beings has shifted from a symbiotic one to a predatory one. In his changed form, the Buyer approaches the supervisor, making a "*Schlup . . . schlup, schlup*" sound (16). Later the Buyer is found "on the nod in the D.S.'s chair," like a snake who descends into an almost comatose snake after ingesting another life form whole. No one can find the district supervisor, and the judge states that it is obvious that he has "in some unspeakable manner uh . . . assimilated the district attorney. However, with no evidence—not even a body—the judge orders his release, and the Buyer achieves his final metamorphosis: "Like a vampire bat he gives off a narcotic effluvium, a dank green mist that anesthetizes his victims and renders them helpless in his enveloping presence. And once he has scored he holes up for several days like a gorged boa constrictor" (17). Ultimately he gets caught assimilating the narcotics commissioner and gets incinerated via flamethrower like nothing more than a feral animal, a condition into which he has either ascended or descended, depending on one's point of view.

The Bradley the Buyer routine serves as an early turning point in the novel that indicates this is not the usual hard-boiled fare of Hammett or Chandler, and the distasteful, nasty incidents will only increase and grow more foul as the novel progresses. Still the narrative seems to remain coherent and linear as Lee goes on the lamb—a criminal phrase that derives from Odysseus's deceitful escape from Polyphemus—throughout the southern United States, which at times scans like an apocalyptic backdrop, demonstrating the hellish nature of the modern world. *Naked Lunch*'s early sections follow Lee as he flees south through Louisiana and Texas and down into Mexico City, replicating the journey in Burroughs's first trilogy of novels as well as in his own life. *Naked Lunch* then jumps to a new section entitled "Benway," in which the narrator and Dr. Benway oversee operations in a fictional place called the Freeland Republic. Thus the linear, quest-like narrative breaks down as the narrator flees off into the night only to reappear in a fictional space where the entire tone of the novel will shift into one of science fiction and horror. Whether Lee is even still the narrator remains a matter of debate since the novel is meant to be read as a series of collage-like routines, and his name never gets mentioned. Instead of a quest with a resolution like Odysseus's, this is a collage that rivals Bosch's panoramic image of Hell in his triptych *The Garden of Earthly Delights* or Michelangelo's fresco *The Last Judgment,* the must less discussed altar painting in the Sistine Chapel. Both paintings feature little corners of horror, and *Naked Lunch* does the same; an overall scene of Sadean delight and despair features innumerable moments of more intimate terrors. However, before these hellish landscapes, the nature of the horror that Burroughs uses in his works needs to be examined.

"Most distasteful thing I ever stood still for": Body Horror in *Naked Lunch*

Naked Lunch opens like a rehash of *Junky* albeit in a more poetic, exaggerated, and funny style—it even recycles elements directly from *Junky* such as the "white trench coat." *Naked Lunch* picks up the posthuman themes from Burroughs's earlier works and develops them into full-fledged body horror. Body horror is a hybrid genre of art that generally blends elements of science fiction and horror together and pursues themes of bodily mutation, dissolution, or infestation. Mary Shelley's gothic classic *Frankenstein; or, The Modern Prometheus* (1818) serves as a major precursor of body horror with its depiction of the construction and reanimation of a living human being from spare body parts. Bram Stoker's *Dracula* (1897) lays further groundwork for the genre with its depiction of a creature (the vampire) who transforms someone via his penetrative bite. The novel can be read as a commentary on the Victorian epidemic of syphilis, another condition spread through a penetrative act. Body horror began to truly take on a definite form in the early twentieth century with H. P. Lovecraft and the circle of authors that he inspired: Robert E. Howard, Clark Ashton Smith, Arthur Machen, and others. Publishing in the pulp magazine *Weird Tales,* these authors created a new hybrid genre termed "weird fiction," which blended elements of fantasy, science fiction, and horror. Lovecraft developed what is commonly known as the "Cthulhu Mythos" in which an ancient race of godlike aliens waits just beyond the veil of existence. Lovecraft's tales feature stories of reanimated corpses, creatures that defy logic to the point of causing insanity, and monsters such as the shoggoths that can constantly mutate their form. Authors continue to write stories set in the Cthulhu mythos well after Lovecraft's death, and Burroughs's makes Lovecraft's importance clear when he mentions Cthulhu (with a slightly different spelling) in the "Invocation to the Ancient Ones" (itself a phrase that hearkens back to Lovecraft) that opens *Cities of the Red Night*. The genre reached its zenith in cinema during the 1970s and 1980s with the early works of David Cronenberg, David Lynch's *Eraserhead* (1977), Ridley Scott's *Alien* (1979), John Carpenter's *The Thing* (1982), and Shinya Tsukamoto's *Tetsuo: The Iron Man* (1988).

Naked Lunch features constant examples of body horror. One cannot discuss Burroughs without talking about "The Talking Asshole" routine, probably his most famous piece of writing. The routine concerns a performer whose asshole learns to talk on its own in a flatulent tone of voice. The asshole soon begins to take over the man as the singular spokesman. Slowly a film grows over the man's mouth and silences him, leaving the asshole as the sole speaker.

A play on the performer-and-dummy shtick, the routine presages the *Alfred Hitchcock Presents* episode and enumerable stories and movies that feature plots of dummies taking over their masters. Here the asshole renders the performer into the dummy, incapable of speech. In many ways the piece suggests that humans are all "talking out of their asses," that language itself proves incapable of expressing anything meaningful and hence that humans are just "nameless assholes," forcing their paltry, shit-ridden ideas on a reality confined by their socially constructed perceptions. In this routine the man devolves—he devolves from a conscious individual into an actual asshole. Generally the asshole is only capable of excretion and possible insertion as happens constantly throughout the novel, but ultimately the tale suggests that everything we say is shit, that language itself constrains humans and turns them into assholes. Humanity must learn to break free of it, and Burroughs hoped to act as their guide. In *Naked Lunch* he remained content with merely depicting this condition, but in the Nova trilogy and the novels beyond, he began to lead humanity into methods of freeing itself from the constraints of the body and language, of turning the reader from a shit into a Johnson.

One of the other famously hilarious body horror episodes, which Burroughs performed with a pitch-perfect precision during live readings, is "Meeting of International Conference on Technological Psychiatry." The routine involves Dr. Shaffer's presentation of the fully de-anxietized male. Shaffer claims to have eliminated neuroses by discarding the entire body except for "an abbreviated spinal column," rendering all other organs and bones as vestigial as the appendix. The patient gets wheeled into the conference, and his flesh immediately melts away revealing a "monstrous black centipede," suggesting that anxiety exists as part of the human condition, a factor that control uses to keep its subjects in check. When the anxiety is removed, a "monster," according to society's definition, emerges, one that will not conform to the will of control. Here is an early example of Burroughs's belief that the human body represents an evolutionary dead end, a stunted form that must be shed to achieve a higher form of existence. One conference attendee yells, "Fetch gasoline! . . . We gotta burn the son of a bitch like an uppity Nigra!" (88)[1] Contrarily a doctor contests that such behavior might lead to legal trouble; the routine then shifts to a courtroom in which the group is being examined by a prosecutor for the death of the man. This hypothetical courtroom epitomizes the mechanisms of control as the prosecutor attacks the ethics of Dr. Shaffer, claiming he has committed multiple crimes of forcible lobotomy (or "brain rape") as the prosecutor terms it, while also pointing to the absence of the centipede as evidence. As the routine returns from the flashback, the giant centipede is "trashing around the room," to which one of the conference goers exclaims, "Man, that motherfucker's hungry. I'm getting out of here, me." This disgust at the centipede epitomizes society's attitude toward the abject, the uncontrollable. The centipede represents humankind freed from anxiety and neurosis, which Deleuze and Guattari argued are instilled in the subject by socioeconomic forces.

Another example of the monstrous or the completely abject is the mugwump, a creature that Cronenberg turned into a major plot point in his adaptation of the novel. A thoroughly abject body, a mugwump feeds on sweets and excretes intoxicating jissom, which has its own cult of addicts. The term "mugwump" actually has a long history and generally means someone who is aloof or apathetic regarding politics and particularly the division into parties. Nothing could better define Burroughs's own political position, which could perhaps be described as libertarian, but even that is rather reductive. The mugwumps in *Naked Lunch* exist not only beyond the dichotomies of liberal and conservative but also beyond the definitions that biopower uses to create and manipulate the subject. The mugwump does not even fit into the category of herbivore or carnivore, for it feeds entirely on sweets. It is pure abjectness. Furthermore not only does it represent abjectivity, but it spreads it by creating abject followers, who like all addicts renounce all social conventions, distinctions, and the like in favor of the drug that fuels them. As Foucault argued, biopower is when power begins to concern itself and to act directly on the human body—body horror, in general, challenges biopower's ability to classify and hence control. The mugwump provides a perfect example because its body refuses categorization, and it spreads its abjectness like a virus—in this case it might be considered a sexually transmitted disease because those infected (the addicts) contract it via the mugwump's ejaculate.

Burroughs has destroyed the boundaries of the body, torn them down to what Deleuze and Guattari termed "the body without organs"; however, as Deleuze and Guattari explained, the body without organs equals death—to strip a body of all organization renders it inert. But Burroughs's body without organs does not occur through a process of slow deterritorialization as Deleuze and Guattari might have envisioned but through a literally visceral detonation in which body parts explode in all directions to take on lives of their own or to mutate to perform new functions. In *Naked Lunch* assholes take on sentience and render the remainder of the body obsolete; thus in this instance one organ assumes command, and the rest of the body becomes vestigial, a body without organs that is used merely as a support system for the asshole. Penises meanwhile become centers of intoxication instead of reproduction. Simultaneously new life forms begin to proliferate: fish boys, and so on. Body horror thus serves a crucial function for Burroughs because it provides examples of absolute abjectivity, beings that refuse all means of categorization and control, hybrid entities that wallow in what society terms filth: assholes; cocks; rectal mucus; unsynthesized drugs that often derive from odious origins; unabashed and rampant promiscuity; orgies; and, of course, homosexuality, an extremely taboo and dirty topic during the supposedly picture-perfect and God-fearing suburbia of 1950s American in which *Naked Lunch* appeared. *Naked Lunch*'s body horror tore down the white picket fences and the perfectly mowed, monoculture lawns to reveal the throbbing cocks, the hungry assholes and cunts, the violent desires, the anticapitalist beliefs, and the queerness that lay caged behind the smiling facades of Beaver Cleaver and Donna Reed. This ejaculation of abjectness, this spewing of seeds of deterritorialization, seems revolutionary; however, the forces of control do not sit idly by as revolution foments. Just as Joseph McCarthy staged a war on communism that labeled certain individuals abject because of their political beliefs, *Naked Lunch* demonstrates how control will always seek to appropriate, contain, and sterilize any outbreak of nonconformity.

Benway; or, How I Learned to Reject Discipline and Embrace Control

The "Benway" section of *Naked Lunch* remains most famous for "The Talking Asshole" routine, but that routine constitutes only a small part that does not even contribute to the plot of the section. The section moves the novel firmly beyond realistic territory and into the sci-fi realm of the mad scientist and the dystopian dictator—Dr. Benway acts as both. There are two different regimes of power in play: discipline versus control. In *Discipline and Punish* Foucault famously demarcated a change of power structures that began in the eighteenth century alongside the Enlightenment. Prior to the eighteenth century, society had operated on the underlying power structure of sovereignty, which used the dictator and the gallows as the spaces from which power emanated throughout society—the church's concept of hellfire and the divine right of kings helped reinforce the impulse to submit and obey. As the Enlightenment progressed, ideas such as social contract theory, particularly in the hands of Locke and Rousseau, began eroding the clout of the sovereign. However, concepts such as freedom and basic rights could not destroy power: as people gained more freedom, power had to decentralize slightly and create multiple sites of indoctrination. The divine right of kings and the infallibility of the church could not keep the entire populace docile any longer—they had to be taught how to obey via new, less apparent channels. Under this regime, which Foucault termed discipline, subjects pass through certain spaces of confinement in their life: schools, prisons, factories, the army barracks, and so on. These spaces require order and cause the subject to internalize the power of discipline without the need for fear and dread that sovereignty required. Paradigms of power do not die overnight—if they ever do completely—so hints of sovereignty would persist into the era of discipline as the transition was increasingly effected during the era of industrialization and the early twentieth century. Despite these vestigial traces, discipline slowly became the order of the day.

For Foucault, Jeremy Bentham's panopticon epitomized the internalization of power under disciplinary regimes. A hypothetical prison, Bentham's space of discipline relies on visibility: a central guard tower resides in a courtyard surrounded by a ring of cells, each of which has a small slit window to the outside. The tower guard can watch only one prisoner at a time, but the prisoners never know when the guard might be focused on them. Therefore the prisoners internalize the gaze of the guard (of discipline) and act as if they are being watched. Eventually a guard may not even be necessary because the idea of one is enough to guide the inmates' behavior. As Dr. Benway says, "the fully functioning police state requires no police." Orwell's *Nineteen Eighty-Four* and Baum's *The Wonderful Wizard of Oz* (1900) demonstrate similar regimes of power—it does not matter if Big Brother or the wizard are real—the citizenry has internalized the belief in their omnipotence. Big Brother acts through his images, a common tactic in real-world totalitarian states, and the wizard functions through the ability to create a similarly visual illusion. The wizard's illusion exists for any individual foolhardy enough to enter his throne room, but it proves unnecessary (most of the time) because, as the populace repeat, "No one sees the wizard."

Benway begins to push away from discipline and toward what Deleuze termed "control societies," a term he takes from Burroughs to indicate the new structure that power has taken during the digital, postmodern era. Discipline distributes power throughout the social grid to enact power from various specific nodes. Since the nodes were not viewed as pronouncements from "power" as the sovereign's voice had been, they proved more insidious, altering subjects' behavior and instilling power within their psyche without their even realizing it. Although discipline multiplied the sites of power's influence, it was still deficient because power was encoded in the subject only at certain spaces along the social grid and because the mechanisms of power were still visible to the critical observer. To be truly efficient, power had to spread itself out, to decentralize itself entirely to encompass the entire social grid, to render every site a space of power. Gilles Deleuze theorized the society of control as the logical progression of Foucault's discussion of power regimes. In their collaborative works, Michael Hardt and Antonio Negri expanded on Deleuze's short essays on the subject to trace the inner workings of control as a global power structure and the possibilities of resistance against it. The concept of control evolves over Burroughs's different conceptualizations of it and his experiments with revolutions and utopian establishments.

Naked Lunch features numerous images of control—junk provides the most obvious choice since the subject willingly submits to a force that dictates his or her behavior. However, the novel's depiction of control proves much more nuanced than the mere metaphorical equation of "junk equals control." But Dr. Benway goes even further by creating conditioning sites as well as spreading the reach of power beyond these sites and into the homes of the general populace, thus beginning the process of decentralization necessary for a genuine control society. Benway's plan to achieve total control over the populace backfires because his methods remain too overt—to follow along with Benway's own statement, the police remain too visible. Thus his plans lead to an obvious society of oppression, and the citizens revolt. As with the devolution of any regime, the tourists attempt to flee Freeland by any means necessary. Fearing the loss of tourist revenue and the ensuing diminishment of authority as a result, the Freeland chamber of commerce issues a statement: "Please to be restful. It is only a few crazies who have from the crazy place outbroken" (38). This banal statement parodies governmental attempts to calm the populace, to maintain the facade of functionality, and to reassert their right of authority. However, their model of power (discipline) cannot ultimately survive the attack of the revolutionaries who use the decentralized tactics of the swarm to destroy or defile every major institution and symbol of Freeland's power and Dr. Benway's schemes. They utilize scatological tactics that use the abject status to which they have been demeaned and reclaim their subjecthood. Essentially Freeland allows a beginning of contemplating the ways in which abjectivity might be used to achieve revolutionary means

The Carnivalesque: Space of Freedom or Control?

Benway's various projects constitute spaces of absolute order and control—to control the populace, one provides them not with shackles but with a perfect order that guarantees they behave in a certain way—as Deleuze argued, one controls by building highways that present the illusion of freedom. Benway's experiments often remain stilted at the level of discipline because they are confined to particular sites, but he begins to try and spread control into the habitus, thus overlaying both public and private spaces with the control grid: a Gestapo-style police force or hospital staff (the two become almost interchangeable under the regime of biopower). Ultimately his attempt to perfectly reorder the populace of Freeland fails because the entire space devolves back into a Hobbesian state of nature. Benway's attempts at perfect control end up negating even the basic social contract and returning people to the state of nature, a state of war, of all against all.

The character of A.J. provides a sharp contrast to Benway because he uses his wealth to inscribe spaces of absolute freedom, chaotic spaces in which even the basest of human desires are played out as party games. He and his entourage also use their wealth to infiltrate high society to completely disrupt the order that the so-called good citizens require. A.J. refuses the social contract in his constant quest for new pleasures (or "kicks" as Kerouac would term them) and amusements. A.J. and his entourage become a roving Sadean space that crashes through society like a whirlwind, creating pop-up (to use today's lingo) spaces of sexual, violent, and scatological disorder. His party represents the carnivalesque—a special type of space in which, as Mikhail Bakhtin explained, the normal rules of society are suspended. The section entitled "A.J.'s Annual Party" provides a perfect example and remains one of the most infamous sections of the book. A true carnival space of drugs, sex, and death, the party requires its participants to check their inhibitions (and perhaps even their lives) at the door. Here sexual desire reaches its absolute limit (except perhaps for the schlupping that Burroughs so ardently desires) as death or murder becomes the pinnacle of sexual achievement among the more quotidian fucking taking place in the orgiastic sea of the party. Awash in a sea of cum, shit, and rectal mucus (a substance that Burroughs mentions throughout his writings), the partygoers can only reach for one more extreme—blood. Sade, of course, introduced pain into the sexual equation with his depictions of sadistic beatings, tortures, sewed-up vaginas, and so on, and Burroughs expanded on this space by introducing the gallows as a feature of the party. Burroughs—or the narrator (the distinction ceases to matter)—remained fascinated with the idea that the body ejaculates as the victim's neck breaks or he or she strangles to death. This leads not just to youths who request each other to hang them, so they can experience the final frontier of orgasms, but also to necrophilia. In one scene a woman cuts a hanged man down and rides his postmortem erection to her own climax. Thus the climax of death becomes the climax of cumming as well—a true moment of *jouissance* in which pleasure slides into pain, a moment in with Eros (the erotic drive) collides and merges with Thanatos (the death drive) into an act that pushes the carnivalesque to its very limit.[2] Real carnivals allow their celebrants to engage in all manner of typically forbidden behavior: public intoxication, public nudity and sex, and so on; however, they generally stop short of murder, a statute that A.J. erases in his anarchic celebration. The *Naked Lunch* buffet is open, and all forms of delight are available if one can stomach the fare—one must be ready to accept what resides at the end of one's metaphorical fork waiting to be consumed but perhaps also waiting to consume the eater. A.J.'s party constitutes a space of absolute abjection, completely free from the strictures of control, but A.J. proves unsatisfied—he delights in spreading abjectness directly into the faces of the upper classes. A.J.'s acts of abjection, then, have little impact on class hierarchies or power structures other than to lampoon them. His acts lack vision and hence cannot achieve any kind of true revolutionary praxis.

"No glot," "clom Friday" . . . Can We Stop "waiting for the man"?

One of the first albums to address the subject of heroin addiction (in addition to transgender issues, sadomasochism, and so on), *The Velvet Underground and Nico* remains one of the most classic underground albums of all time. One of the album's most famous songs, "Waiting for the Man," describes the space of anticipation in which the junkie exists, constantly waiting for the dealer that can fill his lack. Burroughs describes how junkies can be spotted by the fact that they place a napkin under their coffee cup because this indicates a person who has spent a lot of time waiting in coffee shops or cages; that is, "waiting for the man." The Velvets' song distills the relationship between dealer and user down to this one state of being: waiting. As the song says, "The first rule is that you always have to wait." As Burroughs makes clear, this applies not just to junkies but to all people. Why does "the man" keep the other person waiting? To signify that he is always in charge—it is an old-school power move in which "the man" asserts his absolute authority over the junkie. The junkie's life depends on him, so he is forced back into a sovereign regime of power, thus rendering the abject junkie back into a subject. His state of abjectivity persists only if he possesses junk. For that short space of time, he is free of the constraints of subjectivity. However, he always must return to the coffee shop, the place where sovereign power is reasserted as the junkies sit with napkins under their coffee cups, waiting for the man, waiting for the junk to "clom Friday," a spelling Burroughs frequently used to approximate the broken English of Chinese American drug dealers.

CHAPTER 4

Rub Out the Word

The Nova Trilogy and the Severing of the Signifier

There is perhaps only one other trilogy of novels that inspires as much trepidation in the reader of contemporary literature as Burroughs's Nova trilogy (or Cut-Up trilogy, as some critics label it)—Samuel Beckett's trilogy: *Malloy, Malone Dies,* and *The Unnamable.* Beckett's goal in his trilogy is not so different from Burroughs's. Although Beckett did not attack language at its base, he did stage an assault that, over the course, of the three novels eradicates the very form of the novel. *Malloy* starts off the trilogy with an aesthetic and narrative that seems to read like absurdist fare in the vein of Kafka; however, by *The Unnamable* Becket has annihilated every trace of plot, characters, and so on. *The Unnamable* unmoors the reader from all traditional elements of fiction. Beckett provided perhaps the most profound example of stream of consciousness since the novel consists entirely of a disembodied consciousness. Even Joyce's *Finnegans Wake* has a sort of key to understanding its cycles, but Beckett offered no such comfort—the work takes the reader beyond the edges of the page. Burroughs proceeded even further by burning the very pages as they are left behind. The Nova trilogy plays like scorched earth—the meaning of each page gets destroyed as the reader flips to the next one. Stability constantly retreats from the reader's grasp as language tears itself apart.

Naked Lunch showed Burroughs reaching beyond the confessional form so beloved by the Beat Generation and placed him firmly in the echelon of the literary avant-garde; his experiments—collectively known as the cut-ups—over the next decade pushed him beyond the pale of where other writers had dared to go. The story of surrealist painter Brion Gysin's discovery of the infamous cut-up technique has become a mythopoetic moment in the history of the Beat Generation, the avant-garde, surrealism, and postmodernism. The moment also constitutes a turning point in Burroughs's writings in which his works distance themselves from the Beat aesthetic and mark his full transition into avant-garde experimentalism and surrealism. The trilogy also demonstrates Burroughs moving beyond a lingering modernist aesthetic and into distinctly postmodern territory. The cut-up technique was presaged by Dadaist Tristan Tzara, who once created a poem by pulling words out of a hat, an event he discussed in his essay "To Be a Dadaist Poet." The technique that Gysin and Burroughs developed was much more sophisticated than Tzara's random assembly of words, which amounts to little more than refrigerator magnet poetry. However, Tzara and his fellow Dadaists broke the boundaries that allowed future artists such as Gysin and Burroughs to have fertile ground in which to gestate their new methodologies.

Gysin's "Eureka!" moment came when he passed a razor blade through several pages of newspaper and discovered that rearranging the cut-up sections produced interesting results. Gysin began experimenting with the technique, and Burroughs immediately recognized similarities to the style he had already toyed with in *Naked Lunch*. He had hundreds of pages left over from the so-called Word Hoard from which *Naked Lunch* was culled. Burroughs experimented with the cut-up method in collaborative works with Brion Gysin and others—these works give examples while also providing a theoretical framework. Burroughs then took the cut-up method and the attendant philosophy that he developed from it and unleashed it on his own writings. Combining already written material with new material, Burroughs embraced the cut-up method as an ideology as well as an aesthetic that he unleashed on countless multimedia experiments.

Undoubtedly the cut-ups remain Burroughs's most experimental and difficult series of works. To begin with, establishing the trilogy's connection to *Naked Lunch* and a standard edition of each novel proves almost impossible. The first volume of the trilogy, *The Soft Machine,* epitomizes these problems. For starters Burroughs originally claimed that *The Soft Machine,* which at the time still had no title, was a sequel to *Naked Lunch*. In fact it was even staged as part of a separate trilogy by combining sections from *Naked Lunch, The Soft Machine,* and *The Ticket That Exploded* into a new narrative entitled *Dead Fingers Talk* (1963). Furthermore Burroughs substantially revised *The Soft Machine* with each new edition, so there is actually a trilogy of "Soft Machines," as Oliver Harris pointed out in his introduction to the restored edition of *The Soft Machine*. As Harris pointed out, the first edition of *The Soft Machine* was

Burroughs's most radical presentation of cut-ups, and the subsequent editions attempted to make it more palatable to readers desiring a "straight narrative." The second edition remains the one that most readers are familiar with, but in use here is Harris's restored editions of all three cut-up novels, and with *Naked Lunch* treated as a completely separate entity from the cut-ups because, while characters and themes reappear from *Naked Lunch,* the cut-up novels develop their own mythos completely distinct from *Naked Lunch*. Finally the Nova trilogy distinguishes itself from *Naked Lunch* because the latter only depicts the means of control—the Nova trilogy begins to imagine the way out. However, the cut-ups extend far beyond Burroughs's trilogy to include collaborative works with other authors as well as film, audio, and photography experiments. For Burroughs the cut-ups became a multimedia experiment that lasted for a decade and included his friends Brion Gysin (the visual artist and former surrealist) and Ian Sommerville (a mathematician and Burroughs's lover) in the process.

Unleashing His "Word Hoard": Early Cut-Up Experiments

The earliest published collection of cut-ups was *Minutes to Go,* a small-print collection of writings from William S. Burroughs, Brion Gysin, Gregory Corso, and Sinclair Beiles that briefly outlines the methodology for readers before jumping into a series of different examples. The book was really Burroughs and Gysin's project with Corso and Beiles brought on board to demonstrate how the technique could be appropriated by other authors. The anthology features no narratives; instead it begins by showing how texts from newspapers can be cut up to form new stories or to create poetry. Then the book proceeds to cut up more literary texts—Corso and Burroughs cut up Rimbaud, and Burroughs cut up his own words. Corso's poetic contributions prove interesting only as examples of the technique—they pale in comparison to the author's own complex poetics. Beiles's contributions are like Burroughs's: articles taken from magazines or newspapers that are cut up and rearranged to create poems and prose pieces. Gysin's pieces provide little pleasure in reading because of their purely formal nature. For example in one piece he takes a series of words and cuts it up into all its possible permutations to demonstrate how many meanings can proliferate from a small set of words. The book also features cut-ups of St. Mark, Lao Tzu, Francois Rabelais, and Tacitus, which again prove to be of only theoretical interest. Ultimately *Minutes to Go* turns out to be lacking in today's postmodern era, but it was an important opening salvo of a new approach to language, an approach epitomized by the phrase "rub out the word," a phrase that will become a refrain throughout the Nova trilogy.

The Exterminator, another limited-run publication, takes its name from Burroughs's time working as an exterminator in Chicago, but its title also hints toward the extermination of the linear logic and narrative that the cut-up process enacts. Gysin also collaborated on this project, and *The Exterminator*'s title page features an epigraph that lays out the scope of the book's project and the meaning of its title: "Let petty kings the name of party know / Where I come I kill both friend and foe." This couplet (one of the most hackneyed of literary structures) demonstrates the cut-up method's range of influence—it destroys all distinctions, particularly those between good and evil and high and low art. Much critical ink and academic ire has been spilt over postmodernism's blending of high and low art, an approach that Burroughs certainly adopts (earlier than most experimental writers). Some have celebrated this revolution in the arts in which the canon was broken open and the heights of the literary hierarchy were brought down to the same level as pulp fiction. Did John Milton really deserved a higher position than Hugo Gernsback, Jim Thompson, or Stephen King? While this was liberating to some, others saw it as the death knell of art as well as a sign of a major social upheaval in which values become relative and facts lose their certainty.

The Exterminator is more coherent than *Minutes to Go,* which is haphazard at best, and it opens with a more thorough explanation of the cut-up method and its implications. *The Exterminator* opens with the statement, "The Human beings are strung lines of word associates that control 'thoughts feelings and apparent sensory expressions.' . . . See and hear what They expect to see and hear because The Word Lines keep thee in slots."[1] Here Burroughs tied the practice of cut-ups directly into the definition of the human (if there is a stable one), and his lines recall Jacques Lacan's definition of the signifier: "The signifier signifies the subject for another signifier." The subject becomes nothing more than part of the signifying chain, the Word Line as Burroughs called it, which describes and establishes the subject in the overall chain of signification. Signifiers (or words, to be crudely reductive) have meaning only in relation to one another—there is no signified—and the subjects remain trapped in this line of signification in which humanity proves incapable of defining themselves. The control system decides which signifiers to apply to which subjects, but the subjects are still not signifieds—they remain nothing more than another signifier in the computer banks of control in which everyone gets reduced to yet another binary system of ones and zeros. The cut-ups offer a new opportunity to abjectify signification: to topple meaning and authorship from not only the top of art's throne but also from control. The Word Lines constitute one of the major lines of control—images function as another vein of control. In *The Exterminator* Burroughs and Gysin call for an all-out attack on these two intertwining lines of control, and the Nova trilogy begins to demonstrate the method while also using narrative, albeit cut-up narrative, to show the revolutionary potential of the method. The book describes the method and, like *Minutes to Go*, features cut-up prose pieces from Burroughs and what might be called "permutation poems" from Gysin: text that is arranged like a poem but in which each line consists of the same set of words rearranged through all their possible permutations to visually display the signifier's slipperiness. While this feels like more of the same experiments, the book concludes with a series of Gysin's calligraphy pieces, artworks that appear to be language somewhere between the word and image. Upon closer inspection it can be seen that they do not derive from any real language. Gysin follows in the calligraphy tradition, which pays attention to the visual aesthetic of written language, but his visuals go further. The symbols often serve as slight augmentations of one another, thus again demonstrating Gysin's concept of permutational meaning. They blur the line between image and word and further undermine the stability of meaning and the possibility of genuine communication without any slippage. The point of the cut-ups, whether they are textual or visual, is to expose such holes in the word and image lines, to open up lines of flight, as Deleuze would term them, through which revolutionary potential becomes possible.

The final theoretical statement on the cut-ups came with *The Third Mind*, a book by Burroughs and Gysin whose publication was repeatedly delayed, mostly because of its inclusion of illustrations, the same issue that would later haunt Burroughs and McNeill's graphic novel *Ah Pook Is Here*. The book's title refers to Burroughs and Gysin's belief that collaboration between two authors' minds can result in a "third mind" capable of producing ideas and text that neither could produce on his own. Deleuze and Guattari shared a similar belief in their joint publications, but they never designated which writer produced which sections of the books. Burroughs and Gysin always make it clear who authored which parts, thus somewhat undermining the idea of the third mind. *The Third Mind* was finally published in 1978, long after Burroughs had left the cut-ups behind in search of new aesthetics. What the reader gets is a compromised version of their intended book, a mishmash of interviews, theoretical statements, examples of cut-up images and texts, Gysin artworks, and more permutations. The permutations in *The Third Mind* were also aided by mathematician and Burroughs's lover Ian Sommerville.

During the cut-up period, Burroughs produced an enormous amount of writings, scrapbooks, tape-recording experiments, and even films (with the aid of Antony Balch). Most of the works were frustrating to his publishers because they featured zero narrative and were completely unmarketable. In 1984 some of these disparate minor works that had been appeared in small journals or private printings were collected in an anthology from City Lights Press, Lawrence Ferlinghetti's San Francisco–based publishing company. The collection features some examples that are not present in the earlier cut-up books. *The Burroughs File* provides not only cut-up texts such as *The White Subway, The Old Movies, The Retreat Diaries,* and the autobiographical *Cobble Stone Gardens* but also selections from the cut-up scrapbooks, which demonstrate Burroughs's photomontage technique in which he combined photos with handwritten or typed texts to create new associations in the reader's mind. The collection also provides examples of Burroughs three-column method, in which he took strips from three different texts and laid them in columns next to each other. He would then read horizontally across the three texts to produce the cut-ups. More of the cut-up experiments have become available in other recently published studies, but the most profound statement of the cut-up method remains the trilogy of novels that simultaneously demonstrates the technique, explains it, and features a narrative about alien infiltration that literalizes the ideas of control and the cut-up method as means of revolution. While "literalized" may seem to be a misplaced word here, it is apropos because, during his time in the Beat Hotel with Gysin and Sommerville, Burroughs descended into a paranoid state in which he believed his own stories of conspiracy to be true.

"The muttering sickness": The Viral Word in *The Soft Machine*

Of the three cut-up novels, *The Soft Machine* features the most convoluted publication history and editorial difficulties in creating a standard text. At present there are four distinct versions of the novel. The first version was radically experimental, almost all cut-ups, and readers found it almost impossible to read. Disappointed at the reception, Burroughs inserted large sections of "straight narrative" as he always termed it and created the second version of the novel, the one that was most readily available until recently. A third edition appeared featuring more additions, deletions, and revisions, but this version was never the preferred edition when later reprintings began. Finally Oliver Harris undertook the task of untangling the history and various versions of the novel and created a fourth "restored" edition that tries to replicate Burroughs's intentions with the novel while also providing a critical apparatus that includes additional material. Harris's "restored text" is used unless otherwise noted.

Originally Burroughs considered *The Soft Machine* a sequel to *Naked Lunch,* and indeed it came from the same mass of writing. *The Soft Machine* opens, like *Junky* and *Naked Lunch,* with junkies; indeed the first chapter could easily be transferred to one of those novels with its depictions of junkies working the hole (robbing junkies on the subway). In fact many passages repeat themselves from earlier works, once again supporting Burroughs's claim that all his works constitute one large book—Burroughs recycled phrases and stories throughout his career. Most of the chapter "Dead on Arrival" will seem almost like a direct repetition of passages from *Junky* and *Naked Lunch,* but the end of the chapter throws the reader for a loop when it cuts up the previous narrative to create potential new meanings. In fact the harvesting of material from his previous works proves another demonstration of the cut-up technique in action: co-opting other texts and reusing them for new purposes.

The title *The Soft Machine* refers to the human body, a machine made of flesh and fluid but a machine that still functions like any other. Burroughs's discussion of viruses applies to the biological agents but can easily be extrapolated to include computer viruses as well. It can certainly be considered a kind of cybernetic machine with the DNA representing the coding—instead of a binary system (two possible digits: 0 or 1), such as the foundational coding of computer software, DNA relies on a quaternary system (four base amino acids: adenine, cytosine, guanine, or thymine). Viruses constitute little more than protein shells designed to inject their DNA into the body, thus infecting the machine and causing changes. For Burroughs words and images constitute the two viruses that have infiltrated the human host, resulting in alterations in the body's software and hence affecting the behavior of the body's hardware (or wetware, as some later cyberpunk authors might term it).

The cut-up novels conceive of reality as a film (a combination of word and image) that controls the subject's perceptions and actions. Those seeking revolution and a return to parasite-free existence must determine methods of dismantling this film and the forces that have programmed it. The reality film controls human perception through innumerable methods. Control is not some single entity that must be combated—it is not the Galactic Empire versus the Rebel Alliance in *Star Wars* (1977). Comprising corporations, governmental bodies, media, and so on, control is ubiquitous and global—it transcends nation-states and influences humans' most basic perceptions of reality. "The Public Agent" section concerns an operative who remains ignorant of his employer's identity and "get[s] [his] instructions from street signs, newspapers and pieces of conversation" (25). The public agent can parse through the chaotic manifold of sensory input—a type of input that only proliferates as the media society becomes ever more omnipresent—to find the instructions that his employers have left behind. Presently his job consists of tracking down "blue movies of James Dean before the stuff gets to those queers supporting a James Dean habit." Here Burroughs again demonstrated how anything can develop into an addiction whether it is heroin or pornographic films of James Dean. In fact the lines presage the increasing occurrence of pornography addicts in the digital age as well as the fascination with celebrities' sex videos or images that are floating around in cloud servers just waiting for a hacker smart (or lucky) enough to find them.

This agent serves control and has been ordered to root out abjectivity by raiding public restrooms and bathhouses to beat and murder gay men. Ironically the agent, then, descends into junk sickness and uses a Chinese restaurant's restroom to shoot up. The well-behaved subject of control often contains its own secret form of abjectivity; however, his employers offer him a way out of his situation because a drug addict is still better than "a fucking nance." The agent has exceeded his narcotic dosage as prescribed by the Treasury Department, but he is offered the opportunity to kick his habit to avoid trouble; after all, he "ha[s] a wife and kids" like any good, heterosexual, white male subject" (27). The chapter mentions TRAK for the first time but does not delve into this agency of control quite yet; however, the agent does receive directions from the "Home Office" about the "Human Issue." The agent explains that there are "engineering flaws" in humans, so his job consists of "getting it off the shelves and that is what I do. We are not interested in individual models, but in the mold, the human die" (29). According to the computations of control, not all models are flawed, but models such as homosexuals must be eradicated. The section ends with the agent's explaining that he is running out of time, one of control's methods of exerting power and the primary obstacle to human evolution. As an agent devoted to maintaining his status as a loyal subject without dying, he must undergo a "Time Milking" to preserve his life. Even control's agents must submit to control's restrictions. The agent has been tasked with destroying otherness, abjectivity, and queerness. Burroughs, on the other hand, wanted to teach the reader how to queer "the whole deal," to utilize the abject as a means of breaking control lines.

The "TRAK, TRAK, TRAK" chapter opens with brief hints of narrative before transitioning into cut-ups that splice old Burroughs material together with new prose: the return of "no glot," "working the hole," and so on. The chapter then shifts into more "straight narrative" form, to use Burroughs's term, but continues to use hyphens instead of periods and does not follow standard rules of grammar. Comprising largely sentence fragments, the section presents the narrative as a series of actions and images that unfold for the reader in staccato fashion, thus undermining the necessity of syntax, grammatical structure, and logical paragraph progression. Burroughs's cut-ups decimate the page like machine-gun fire: images and actions assault the reader in rapid, full-auto succession, blending new material together with text that has appeared previously in this book or earlier in Burroughs's corpus. Of course Burroughs's cut-ups frequently feature text from other writers as well, text that can range from newspaper clippings to Shakespeare. This willful plagiarism further challenges the reader's idea of an independent author and suggests that texts can be understood only in an intertextual fashion; that is, no author's work can be called truly original—it plagiarizes from and participates in other literary traditions that must also be considered. Therefore the permutations of potential meanings in Burroughs's cut-ups spiral "off the page in all directions." The cut-ups constitute an attack on language, literature, and the possibility of creating meaningful utterances. The cut-up savages the reader with prose that is at times almost impenetrable, and in other moments it achieves an almost poetic aesthetic that revels in the beautiful and the horrific alike.

In cut-up fashion Bill, the narrator, describes an almost apocalyptic background against which he and his lover Joselito travel. The passage takes lines from *Naked Lunch* and lines that will repeat throughout the cut-ups to depict a world of control filled with the refuse of humankind as well as new posthuman mutations. They travel "through customs checks and control posts" and eventually wind up

> on the edge of Yage country where shy Indian cops checked our papers. Through broken stellae, pottery fragments, worked stones, condoms and shit-stained comics, slag heaps of phosphorescent metal excrement—Faces eaten by the pink and purple insect disease of The New World—Crab boys with human legs and genitals crawl out of clay cubicles—Terminal junkies hawk out crystal throat gristle in the cold mountain wind—Good ball bums covered with shit sleep in rusty bathtubs—A delta of sewage to the sky under terminal stasis, speared a sick dolphin that surfaced in bubbles of coal gas—Taste of metal left silver sores on our lips—Only food for this village built on iron racks over an iridescent lagoon—swamp delta to the sky lit by orange gas flares. (33)

As can be seen in this example, even a single paragraph of cup-up writing contains an almost impossible amount of information. Here is the ultimate blurring of the lines between nature and culture. The natural world and the world of metal have become fused into a hybrid that destroys or mutates the life forms within it—boys that are half-crab, dolphins swimming in coal gas, metallic air, new insect diseases; and the humans—presumably a product of nature—become so infiltrated by this metallic world that they shit phosphorescent metal. Aside from the metal, this is also a world of refuse, a garbage dump navigated by new forms of life seeking evolutions that will allow them to prosper in their new postnatural environment. This ubiquitous trash dump parallels Philip K. Dick's depiction of "kipple" in *Do Androids Dream of Electric Sheep?* (1968), garbage that seems to proliferate without any discernible origin as if it grows on its own. The agents of control are still present, but humanity seems to be heading closer and closer to its evolutionary dead end and possibly the dead end of the planet as well. Adaptation remains a mere tool of survival—perhaps the crab-boys' new forms allow them to breathe the metallic air and to swim in the coal gas ponds without harm, yet they remain trapped in the stasis of this world that Burroughs reiterated at several points in the above passage. To move beyond stasis, life forms must evolve beyond the dying environment around them and the control machinery that both constricts them and allows this environmental catastrophe to escalate more and more.

To demonstrate how control's power extends beyond governmental agents and bodies like the "customs checks" mentioned above, Burroughs introduces the reader to the TRAK company, a company with countless subsidiaries and a long, bizarre history, a company that seeks a totalized form of monopoly akin to the ubiquitous nature of control. Unlike the petty monopolies of Carnegie, Rockefeller, and Ma Bell, TRAK's idea of a total monopoly extends not just to their products, the servicing of these products, and their distribution but also to infiltrating power itself to the point where government and corporation become indistinguishable—one of the major characteristics that would become a central characteristic in cyberpunk, a genre that Burroughs heavily influenced. TRAK's modus operandi gets expressed by an unnamed speaker—presumably an administrator at TRAK: "We sell the Servicing and all TRAK products have precise need of TRAK servicing. . . . This is not just another habit-forming drug this is *the* habit-forming drug takes over all functions from the addict including his completely unnecessary under the uh circumstances and cumbersome skeleton. Reducing him ultimately to the helpless condition of a larva. He may be said then to owe his very life such as it is to TRAK servicing (41)"[2] This passage recalls the de-anxietized male from *Naked Lunch,* but it also draws out a genealogy of power, to use Nietzsche's and Foucault's term, that shows how such power begins to internalize itself in the human psyche.

Before the above speech, all-capitalized ads for TRAK cigarettes appear: "SMOKE TRAK CIGARETTES. THEY LIKE YOU. TRAK LIKE ANY YOU. ANY TRAK LIKE YOU. SMOKE TRAKS. THEY SERVICE. TRAK TRAK TRAK" (37). Cigarettes often get compared to heroin addiction in terms of difficulty to quit. The cigarette gets you hooked into TRAK's control machinery, but that is only the first step. The above advertisement also begins the second stage of one's internalization of TRAK control. By repeating the word "TRAK" frequently and promising a product and company that will accept anyone no matter how abject, TRAK begins to embed its name in the reader's consciousness. TRAK proceeds to transcend the confines of a monopolistic corporation and enter the governmental field as well. As the U.S. populace has learned from a recent series of court decisions, corporations are people; the most famous example of this remains "Citizens United," as it is generally called, which gave corporations the right to unlimited donations to political campaigns, thus giving them the power to influence elections in a way that is only dissimilar to TRAK's in its subtlety. The TRAK Reservation develops—it includes "almost all areas in and about the United Republics of Freeland" (41). A privatized police force run by TRAK—like the privatized police group in Paul Verhoeven's *Robocop* (1987) or the private "armies" the United States has utilized in its recent wars—patrols the reservation, "and no one knows what is and what is not Reservation cases, civil and criminal cases are summarily removed from civilian courts with the simple word TRAK to unknown sanctions" (41–42). The TRAK reservation recalls Franz Kafka's *The Trial,* in which Joseph K. is arrested, tried, and executed for a crime that he never understands.

TRAK has taken over the area's law enforcement and judiciary functions, thus making the company the creator of laws, laws that remain inscrutable to its citizenry. All other companies become anathema as the usage of TRAK products develops into the benchmark of a solid subject. While TRAK seemed completely accepting at first, it now reveals that it divides people along subject/abject lines. The abject refuse TRAK's products and attempt to maintain autonomy in a space where TRAK dictates every aspect of life—they sell a washing machine, they manufacture the clothes to wash and the detergent, and they send the friendly maintenance engineer to fix the product when it experiences problems.

However, to paraphrase Marx, one specter still haunts the TRAK reservation—evolution. Evolution still offers the TRAK citizens the possibility of reclaiming their freedom and shaping new identities. They must not merely adapt—they must become, as Nietzsche would maintain; to break free from the environment keeping them trapped in the stasis of being, of remaining subject to the ruling government and ethics (here an ethics based on consumerism). TRAK, however, strives to close this loophole by guiding humanity's evolution into an even more inescapable dead end by transforming them into larva, not even fully formed creatures, creatures that cannot function autonomously and need TRAK for everything. The narrator addresses this earlier in the chapter: "Make yourself a bit smart—Who is the third that walks beside you to a stalemate of black lagoons and violet light? Last man—Phosphorescent centipede feeding on flesh strung together we are digested and become nothing here" (36). "The third that walks beside you" is taken directly from T. S. Eliot's *The Wasteland* (1922) and is apropos in several ways. First, the chapter takes the reader through a kind of wasteland, one in which nature itself becomes a horror—as Eliot stated in *The Wasteland,* "I will show fear in a handful of dust." Humanity itself has become a wasteland to Burroughs because it is incapable of escaping its evolutionary impasse. The full passage from Eliot reads,

> Who is the third who walks always beside you?
> When I count, there are only you and I together
> But when I look ahead up the white road
> There is always another one walking beside you
> Gliding wrapt in a brown mantle, hooded
> I do not know whether a man or a woman
> —But who is that on the other side of you?

For Burroughs, of course, the hooded figure could be read as control, a force that is always here but usually masked by media and so on, a force always trying to influence humanity's every move. As Michel de Certeau explained, city planning even tries to prescribe which streets people take on their daily journeys. Deleuze amplified this statement when he said that people are not controlled by something but by building highways, which discreetly control the flow of individuals, commerce, and so on.

The passage from *Soft Machine* also features another reference—whether it is intentional or not (intentionality does not matter to Burroughs anyway)—to the last man, a major concept from Nietzsche's *Thus Spake Zarathustra* (1981). Like Burroughs, Nietzsche believed that the human constitutes only a transitory form that must be cast off to achieve true autonomy; as Zarathustra states, "Man is a rope . . . fastened between animal and Superman—a rope over an abyss." The last man represents humanity's complacent descent into evolutionary stasis, a commitment to static being that precludes any possibility of breaking out of the eternal return of the same—they mourn the demon's words from Nietzsche's *The Gay Science*. The last man is the opposite of the übermensch—the goal that humanity must strive for, a utopian goal of becoming, of breaking free from society's constraints to create one's own sense of ethics. This goal can, of course, be perverted as the Nazis did with Nietzsche's ideas, but the Nazis created a totalitarian society that Nietzsche would have abhorred for its harsh imposition of rules and subject definition. The Nazis found abjects everywhere and executed them in an attempt to create a society of pure subjects, a homogenous society that leads directly to the last man. Nietzsche urged the reader to resist the forces such as those of TRAK or the Nazis that want to create the easily controllable last man; Nietzsche's philosophy leads naturally to the abject. By making oneself abject, one creates one's own rules and shuns the dictates of society, thus allowing the "dividual" to seek out a new ethics—it is important to remember that ethics are still not only possible but crucial when one reaches a state beyond good and evil—uncompromised by the influence of other systems of thought. This does not mean that one can commit murder, as de Sade articulates in the anti-ethical philosophy section of

La philosophie dans le boudoir ("Philosophy in the Bedroom," 1795), because, as Nietzsche stated, beyond good and evil does not mean beyond good and bad. But Kant's categorical imperative cannot be used to mathematically determine ethical decisions. In the TRAK Reservation, one need not worry about ethical decisions—TRAK has made them for the person even if he or she remains unaware of the criteria. TRAK walks beside one, guiding his or her hands and minds, teaching and protecting or punishing the person (if necessary)—remember to be a good little subject and buy TRAK. TRAK seeks to build a society of the last man, one in which the "dividual" has been rendered into a centipede or a larva that can no longer function on its own much less make revolutionary decisions. Burroughs used TRAK to demonstrate how not just governmental bodies interpellate humans into subjects—corporations serve an equally important role as does the media and large portions of the mass-market entertainment industry. With the "TRAK, TRAK, TRAK" chapter, Burroughs laid out the basics of a control society, which he began to flesh out further in *The Soft Machine* while also depicting revolutionary agents fighting against the control machinery. The rest of the cut-up novels will build on this conceptualization and imagine the cut-ups as a method of cutting the lines of control and subverting them.

The most famous routine from *The Soft Machine,* "The Mayan Caper," provides a coherent story for anthologization but also proves essential because it depicts a revolutionary agent fighting the forces of control. Joe Brundige, a journalist writing for the *Evening News,* serves as the narrator, thus tying the story into the media arm of control. Brundige has just returned from a trip back in time about which he provides a warning: "It is precise operation—It is dangerous—It is difficult—It is the new frontier and only the adventurous need apply—But it belongs to *anyone* who has the courage and know-how to enter—It belongs to *you*—" (79).[3] Joe begins his temporal sojourn by applying Burroughs's fold-in method with old newspapers. He explains that readers absorb the entirety of a newspaper's (or other text's) contents even if only subliminally, so folding together old newspapers can take a person back in time. Joe begins adding novels, letters, magazines, and even photographs to the mix. His research leads him naturally to a film studio since films give the illusion of time. Film serves as the natural progression because it presents the illusion of movement and consequently the illusion of temporal progression. Films have been calculated to run at twenty-four frames per second because that most closely approximates "natural" visual perception. The audience actually sits in the dark for most of the projection of a film at a movie theater. Cinema has changed since the introduction of digital photography and video, but we will stick with film as Burroughs knew it because his metaphor relies on it. Really such definitions prove moot since the reality film remains the only plane that most people perceive, a plane that controls their ideas and behavior. Only the daring who have knowledge of cut-ups and fold-ins can crack this surface and reveal the machinery beneath, to run the reality film projector "off track," which becomes a refrain throughout the cut-up novels. When the reality film's projection fails, then the illusion of reality is compromised, much like what one might experience in the older days of cinema: a reel going off track, burn-outs, and so on. Burroughs's reality film recalls Plato's "Allegory of the Cave" in which prisoners in a cave perceive reality only via the shadows projected on the cave wall. The question, then, becomes whether the cave dwellers are better off in their ignorance of the truth, whether they should be rescued and brought to the surface, and whether, if they were rescued, their minds could handle the transition to the surface. Burroughs believed—not just in his fiction but in real life as well—that another reality exists, one in which human evolution becomes a possibility again. Like Nietzsche's Zarathustra, he came to show the way out of time and into space, out of the reality film's control and into a space of endless possibilities.

During his research at the film studio, Joe learns to "talk and think backwards on all levels . . . by running film and sound track backwards" (80). After three months of time travel training, he journeys to Mexico City to study the Mayan civilization. Burroughs was always fascinated with the Mayans, particularly the Mayan codices that still have not been fully deciphered. The narrator explains that the Mayans had three calendars: "a solar, a lunar, and ceremonial calendar rolling along like interlocking wheels" (81). The Mayan calendar stretches from a mythical start date to the end of the world, and "the absolute power of the priests . . . depended on their control of the calendar," on their monopoly over time (81). Next Joe finds a "vessel" in a young man of Mayan ancestry who is considered a medium (someone who can establish communication between the living and the dead). After taking part in a special ritual, the narrator steps into the ancient Mayan world only to immediately feel the power of the priests: "I felt the crushing weight of evil insect control forcing my thoughts and feelings into prearranged molds, squeezing my spirit in a soft, invisible vise" (88). Unlike disciplinary power, control does not function through programming subjects in certain localized areas but instead studies subject behavior and creates "molds" based on them: worker, overseer, priest, and so on. However, the descriptional parameters can become extremely complex as the control machinery becomes more sophisticated. For example in today's social media age the control machinery can easily tap into the cloud to find out what many subjects ate for breakfast or ogle videos of subjects having sex the night before. They can also label loyal citizens and malcontents—something that President Donald Trump attempted regarding the inauguration protests.

To remain unnoticed by the control machinery, one must try to fit into an acceptable mold that will attract minimal attention: the reporter immediately blends in with the workers, gets assigned a hut by an overseer, and "turned on the thoughts of a half-witted Indian" (88). If Burroughs's imperialistic and racist language is disregarded, which probably should not be done, the passage provides a powerful commentary on a power paradigm that monitors not only outward behavior but interior thoughts as well. In the story the Mayans have telepathy, but the present-day control machine also uses humans' outward behavior to try and derive their internal thoughts. Otherwise how would ads on Facebook know what one wanted to buy on Amazon? Furthermore social media allows users to constantly post their thoughts, thus consciously feeding new data to the control machine, which only creates more perfectly constructed algorithms and heuristic analyses. While society has willingly—and even happily—embedded themselves further and further into the control apparatus, the reporter seeks to make himself invisible to the control agents. He achieves an anonymous state and studies Mayan life, even witnessing some of their brutal punishments such as "*Death in The Ovens*" or "*Death in Centipede*" (88).

During his anonymity Joe constantly records Mayan festivals and rituals. However, his position proves complicated because he cannot play these tapes without risking detection, and he also needs to record the image track because word and image remain inexplicably intertwined as twin data sources for the control machinery. Since humans' idea of the world remains structured by the reality film, then it requires both sound and video—their Tweets and Facebook status updates are just as important as their Instagram photos, their YouTube videos, their Skype sessions, and the memes they post, whether they feature political commentary or lolcats. Brundige learns that the control machine's inventors died without passing on their knowledge, so the current priests would have no way of fixing it should it break down or be sabotaged. After prostituting himself to a priest, who metamorphoses into a crab-man, and using the drug he had acquired before his journey, he manages "to [take] over the priest's body," "[gain] access to the room where the codices were kept, and [photograph] the books" (90–91). He dismantles the control machine by changing dates—harvests occur offseason, and so on—and he begins to cut revolutionary messages into "the control music and festival recordings" (91). Here is witnessed the revolutionary call that will reappear in numerous permutations throughout the trilogy: "Cut word lines—Cut music lines—Smash the control images—Smash the control machine—Burn the books—Kill the priests—Kill! Kill! Kill!" (91).

Now instead of transmitting control signals, the control apparatus orders its subjects to attack the machinery and destroy it. Brundige uses the control mechanisms to tear the system apart from the inside. Revolution breaks out in the fields as the reporter dashes toward the temple with his "camera gun," which "takes and vibrates image to radio static" (91). The final revelation is that "the priests *were* nothing but word and image, an old film rolling on and on with dead actors. Priests and temple guards went up in silver smoke as I blasted my way into the control room and burned the codices" (91). As the old reality film of control disappears, the Mayan world begins to tear itself apart to reveal the reality that the priests had been concealing, the truth not the shadows. The reporter beats a hasty retreat as "tidal waves rolled over the Mayan control calendar" (92). This story features a fictionalized account of tactics that Burroughs believed could be used in real life, such as using tape recorders to incite riots. Burroughs also forecasted the neo-Marxist ideas of Hardt and Negri, who argue that control has spread itself out to encompass the globe and is hence no longer constrained by national borders. Marx and Engels had envisioned capitalism becoming a worldwide phenomenon, a moment at which rebellion became possible on a global scale. However, according to Hardt and Negri, it is control, which is generally linked to capital in one way or another, that has become ubiquitous. Since it has become ubiquitous, then, following Marx's idea, revolution should be possible in a way that it has not been before. But how? Hardt and Negri point to the communication channels with which control has overlaid the global grid—it might be added that the global grid's breakdown gets ever more precise than simple longitude and latitude lines. However, as Burroughs and Deleuze make clear, the forces of control own the communication channels, so their value as revolutionary instruments can easily be compromised.

While "The Mayan Caper" remains the most famous and anthologized section of the novel, "Cross the Wounded Galaxies" has probably sparked the most critical discussions because it depicts a hypothetical origin of language's birth and evolution among the primal waters before humanity arose. The title might confuse first-time readers because it suggests some kind of space opera, but the routine actually concerns the wound that civilizations across the galaxy have all received. That wound is the word—the word is the virus that infects every species capable of speech, and Burroughs showed that the infection has been there since the species' genesis. The story opens with ape forms who contract "the muttering sickness" while passing through frozen "white time caves" (177). Most of these protohumans died there, but the narrator (it is a first-person narrative) "brought the sickness . . . frozen in my throat to hatch in the warm steamlands spitting song of scarlet bursts in egg flesh" (177). The "steamlands" become a space of primordial transformation, and the narrator describes a primal scene of parasitic infection, mutation, shitting, fucking, and murder. The humid swamps provide fertile ground for the sickness to grow and spread to the other apish creatures, who "fell in flesh heaps. Sick apes spitting blood laugh. Sound bubbling in throats torn with the talk sickness. Faces and bodies covered with pus foam. Animal hair thru the purple sex-flesh. Sick sound twisted thru body. Underwater music bubbling in blood beds. Human faces tentative flicker in and out of focus. We waded into the warm mud-water. Hair and ape flesh off in screaming strips. Stood naked human bodies covered with phosphorescent green jelly. . . . Till the sun went and a blue wind of silence touched human faces and hair. When we came out of the mud we had names" (177). Here the language of putrefaction and disease is ineluctably intertwined with evolution. It is the virus that spurs evolution, that causes the decaying of one form and the emergence of another. The passage implies that the transition to "human" occurs only with the birth of language. Now they have names and can name the world around them. Names are one of the first requirements of subjecthood. Following along with Althusser, an individual cannot be interpellated into a subject without someone being able to hail them by a name.

The chapter then offers a brief history of the evolutionary chain from ape forms all the way to Mr. Bradly Mr. Martin, one of the chief centers of control in the trilogy. Images assault the reader of various interstitial stages of humans as they fuck, kill, eat, and spread their sickness through blood, shit, and cum. The chapter becomes fragmented as Burroughs cuts up the narrative—it circles back on itself, alters the story, and inserts new material. Time stretches out: "The years. The long. The many. Such a place" (181). Here Burroughs has given another series of sentence fragments to which the reader must add information to bring them into coherence (or at least his or her own version of coherence). The first three sentence fragments express measurements of time, space, and quantity while the final sentence fragment grounds it in a topographical space. Despite the lack of verbs, these "sentences" still manage to convey a sense of melancholy as people drink piss, cover themselves in shit, and copulate while always spreading the disease.

Finally power appears amid this pandemonium of biology run amok: "Licking the gristle from his laughing teeth and gums I said: 'I am Allah. I made you'" (181). The pronouns get further confused here as the third person slides into the first person, simultaneously linking the animalistic with the divine. One now sets himself apart as a god figure, as the source of life and power—he creates a hierarchy despite being nothing more than a gristle-sucking animal who has learned to use language as a means of exerting power. Language and power immediately become linked, leading to the invocation of Mr. Bradly Mr.

Martin and his board members who run the control machinery. Already a double character, Mr. Bradly Mr. Martin becomes more important as the cut-ups progress. In the chapter's finale, Mr. Bradly Mr. Martin seems to be listening to a report, but this remains debatable since the section appears abruptly in cut-up fashion and then ends with a parenthetical statement. The report involves an "Explosive Bio-Advance," which it makes clear are the ape creatures spontaneously evolving, and the attempt "to employ Electrician in gasoline crack of history," but they "Couldn't reach flesh switch in time." Therefore the evolution of flesh cannot be stopped: "Migrants of ape in gasoline crack of history, explosive bio-advance out of space to neon." The crack in history constitutes a Deleuzian line of flight, an escape hatch through which one can redirect or subvert the path that control has laid down. The electrician has tried to cut the power to the flesh switch, thus closing the possibility of evolution by making the crack invisible. However, he fails to make it in time, so the apes slide through the crack, a gasoline crack because passing through it has the power to set off this explosive bio-advance—it tosses a Molotov cocktail into the evolution machine and radically alters the destiny of the species. Control will ultimately adapt to these changes because more precise language and naming enable control to function more perfectly. This crack in history gets closed, and humankind sinks into static being, an evolutionary impasse held in place with language and the inability to think between either/or Aristotelian logic. Burroughs spent the rest of the series, and indeed his entire career, seeking for another line of flight, another crack in history via which humankind can reignite the evolutionary process and engage in radical becomings. *The Soft Machine* ends with the merging of flesh and language, a language that will label and turn the human body into a machine to be controlled. The utopian ideal then becomes Deleuze and Guattari's "body without organs," a complete refusal of organizational forms that social forces have inscribed on humanity and a willingness to embrace absolute space, a state where the human can stretch out infinitely and define itself anew. With the almost limitless array of information contained in a subject, the number of new definitions becomes more infinite than the entries in Gysin's permutational poems.

Incompatible Life Forms: Uniting the Partisans in *The Ticket That Exploded*

The publication history of *The Ticket That Exploded* is less convoluted than *The Soft Machine*'s because it only appeared in two editions (before Harris's "restored" edition): one in 1962 and another in 1967, which featured 50 percent more material. As Robin Lyndenberg explained, the final version of *The Ticket That Exploded* appeared after Burroughs had begun expanding the usage of cut-ups to audio and video. Consequently "the cut-up effects in *Ticket* seem more controlled, more like the product of a complex machine than of a dream or drug hallucination. Burroughs wields the cut-up method in *Ticket* as a war machine, a linguistic weapon against the binary thinking which generates conflict on a philosophical level (in all either/or antitheses), on a political level (in all civil and interstellar war games), and on a personal level (in all relations, sexual and non-sexual)" (70). Jennie Skerl and Timothy S. Murphy helped explain the difference between *The Soft Machine* and *The Ticket That Exploded.* Skerl maintained that the first novel depicts "social control of mankind throughout human history by the manipulation of bodily needs," hence the novel begins in the present of *Junky* and *Naked Lunch* and ends with a depiction of language's birth (Skerl 52; T. Murphy, *Wising Up the Marks* 108).[4] Thus, as Lyndenberg, Skerl, and Murphy have all argued (to one degree or another), *The Soft Machine* establishes the existing conditions of control and traces them back to the origins of language. In *The Ticket That Exploded,* Burroughs was prepared to wield his newly honed weapon to attack these conditions at their very foundation: language itself. To begin imagining this war machine in action, the reader must finally be acquainted with the unifying story of the trilogy. As Murphy argued, "The basic premise of Burroughs's trilogy does not receive explicit exposition until the second volume. . . . The routine entitled 'the nova police' offers a discursive presentation of the antagonisms between the Nova Mob and its marks, and between the Mob and the Nova Police who pursue it, both of which antagonisms have heretofore appeared only in allusive cut-ups" (*Wising Up the Marks* 109). Therefore attention is due this section of the novel, which appears about a quarter of the way into the novel.

The section introduces readers to Inspector Lee of the Nova Police, who holds a press conference to explain the basic nature of the conflict between the Nova Mob and the Nova Police:[5]

> i doubt if any of you on this copy planet have ever seen a nova criminal—(they take considerable pains to mask their operations) and i am sure none of you has ever seen a nova police officer—When disorder on any planet reaches a certain point the regulating instance scans *police*—otherwise—Sput—Another planet bites the cosmic dust—i will now explain some of the mechanisms and techniques of the nova where are always deliberately manipulated—i am quite well aware that no one on any planet likes to see a police officer so let me emphasize in passing that the nova police have no intention of remaining after their work is done—That is, when the danger of nova is removed from this planet we will move on to other assignments—We do our work and go—(61)[6]

Given Burroughs's intense dislike for all law enforcement, it seems odd that he would cast them as heroes, but the Nova Police assume control only to achieve a desired result and then vanish without any lingering presence to oppress the planet. The nova police seek to assuage the fears of the population about their world becoming another police-oppressed society by promising they will relinquish their power once their objective has been obtained, an objective that does involve the very safety of the planet itself.

In astrophysics the term "nova" refers to an astronomical event in which the interaction of two stars causes the sudden appearance of a bright spot that looks like a new star. Burroughs's usage of the term differs, particularly since he applies it to planets instead of stars, but it remains linked to the original definition. As Inspector Lee explains,

> The basic nova technique is very simple: Always create as many insoluble conflicts as possible and always aggravate existing conflicts—This is done by dumping on the same planet life forms with incompatible conditions of existence—There is of course nothing 'wrong'[7] about any give life form since 'wrong' only has reference to conflicts with other life forms—The point is these life forms should not be on the same planet—Their conditions of life are basically incompatible in present time form and it is precisely the work of the nova mob to see that they remain in present time form, to create and aggravate the conflicts that lead to the explosion of a planet, that is to nova—(62)[8]

Going nova then occurs when conflicting, dichotomous conditions remain in a static condition for too long, resulting in the destruction of the planet.

The Nova Police's job involves tracking the Nova Mob and preventing planets from "going nova." Burroughs ties the Nova Mob's methods directly into his experiments with audio recording. They "record the most violent and threatening statements of group one with regard to group two and play back to group two" (62). The response is then recorded and played for group one, and this "feedback," if left unchecked, leads to "nuclear war and nova" (62). Lee proceeds to list the most wanted members of the Nova Mob, which include individuals such as "Green Tony," "The Brown Artist," "Hamburger Mary," and "The Subliminal Kid." Most important, there is "Mr and Mrs D also known as 'Mr Bradly Mr Martin' also known as 'The Ugly Spirit,' thought to be the leader of the mob" (62–63). "The Ugly Spirit" remains a recurring "character" in Burroughs's fiction as well as a force in his life. As he explained in his introduction to *Queer,* he believed that the Ugly Spirit possessed him when he shot Joan Vollmer. Since that time it had continued to haunt him until it was finally exorcised during a sweat lodge ceremony. The Nova Mob operate in a similar manner—they use individuals as vessels that they possess and use to interact with the world.

As Lee further explains, "nova criminals are not three-dimensional organisms . . . but they need three-dimensional humans to operate—The point at which the controller intersects a three-dimensional human being is known as a coordinate point" (65). Nova criminals always act through a certain type of individual: addict nova criminals use addicts, chain smokers always use smokers, and so on. The criminals can be traced because of these peculiarities, but they generally maintain a line of coordinate points that they can shift between to avoid detection. They cannot just jump from one random body to another, but they can create lines of flight down which they can escape the Nova Police. An arrest can only be made once all coordinate points have been blocked off and the final harboring host discovered. Lee goes on to explain that nova criminals function like viruses—they have an addiction or vice that allows them to infect a host organism that has a similar weakness.

Lee has arrived because the Nova Mob has set up a control machine on the planet and erected a blockade around it. With the aid of Saturnian partisans, the nova police have broken the blockade and begun their arrest operations. Of course they required local agents as well, but most law enforcement agencies were already corrupted, so "paradoxically some of [their] best agents were recruited from the ranks of those who are called criminals on this planet" (64). Thus the conflict between the Nova Mob and the Nova Police inverts Burroughs typical depiction of criminals versus police. Generally the police are corrupt, and the abject, marginal individuals possess a truer sense of ethics. The Nova trilogy scrambles this by having the Nova Mob representing the forces of control while the police work with partisans and criminals to fight the mob's efforts to incite nova. Once Nova Police have cleaned up the planet, the nova criminals will be brought "to the Biological Court" for the indicated alterations" (63). The Biological Court often becomes corrupted as soon as it forms, so they convene on new locations every day to avoid a miscarriage of justice. This is the central war being fought throughout the Nova trilogy whether it is in the background or explicitly discussed. Hints of this story appear throughout *The Soft Machine*, but *The Ticket That Exploded* makes the story clearer, and the story culminates in *Nova Express*.

"Prisoner, come out": *Nova Express* and the Death of the Signifier

Nova Express's publication history proves simple compared to the first two novels because there is only one edition, published in 1964, discounting Harris's "restored" version. *Nova Express* opens with one of Burroughs's most powerful segments, "The Last Words of Hassan i Sabbah," which Burroughs performed with especial force in his readings. A statement of the revolutionary ideals of the entire trilogy, "Last Words" ridicules humanity's pathetic, bureaucratic culture and its hypocritical facade of democracy with the blackest vitriol. The chapter indicts the entire control apparatus, which comprises not just governmental bodies but also corporations; in fact the distinction between the two becomes blurred beyond recognition. Hassan i Sabbah's monologue opens with a call to all the forces of control and proceeds to openly mock them while laying bare the machinery they attempt to hide from the public by proffering the simulacrum of freedom: "Listen to my last words anywhere. Listen to my last words any world. Listen all you boards syndicates and governments of the earth. And you powers behind what filth deals consummated in what lavatory to take what is not yours. To see the ground from unborn feet forever—" (1). Hassan assaults the cowardice of control agents by hypothesizing and mimicking the fears they might be espousing to one another: "Don't let them see us. Don't tell them what we are doing—" (1). Hassan offers this rejoinder: "Are these the words of the all-powerful boards and syndicates of the earth?" Hassan's imagined board members fret over various conspiracies, backroom dealings, and secret technologies, such as "The Cancer Deal with the Venusians." While these conspiracies reside in the science-fictional realm, secret dealings within the U.S. government have been exposed since the 1950s when a U.S. U-2 spy plane crashed in the Soviet Union, proving that the United States was illegally entering Soviet airspace for the purposes of spying. Since then many other shady U.S. secrets have either come to light, been declassified, or been the subject of various conspiracy theories: the alternative theories about JFK's assassination; the assassination of Mohammad Mosaddegh, the elected leader of Iran; the CIA's testing of the psychedelic drug MKUltra on human subjects; the supposed crash of a UFO at Area 51 (a classified site for black projects) in Roswell, New Mexico; the collaboration with and subsequent deposition of Manuel Noriega, the ruler of Panama; the Iran-Contra Affair; and the numerous conspiracy theories surrounding the 9/11 attacks. In the digital era, information becomes available even more quickly, and conspiracy theorists or information disseminators can congregate more easily via websites such as Reddit. Meanwhile some hackers display the extent of control's access to personal information while others, such as Julian Assange and Edward Snowden, have leaked classified information and exposed corruption and misconduct in government agencies such as the NSA. The NSA apparently also enjoys downloading nude pictures of smartphone users when they are scanning communication content (unbeknownst to the public). Much like Assange's Wikileaks, Burroughs's version of Hassan calls for a total exposure of information: "Listen: I call you all. Show your cards all players. Pay it all pay it all pay it *all* back. Play it all play it all play it *all* back. For all to see. In Times Square. In Piccadilly" (2).

Hassan, who serves as Burroughs's mouthpiece in *Nova Express* just as Zarathustra served as Nietzsche's in *Thus Spake Zarathustra,* wants to rip the blinders off the readers' eyes, to publicly reveal control's secrets, and to guide humankind to its next stage of evolution. Hassan claims that the control agents are "traitors to all souls everywhere" and explains how humankind reached its current evolutionary dilemma: "What scared you all into time? Into body? Into shit? I will tell you: '*the word.*' Alien word '*the.*' '*The*' *word* of Alien Enemy imprisons '*thee*' in Time. In Body. In Shit. Prisoner, come out. The great skies are open. I Hassan i Sabbah *rub out the word forever.* In you I cancel all your words forever. And the words of Hassan i Sabbah as also cancel" (3).

Here Burroughs engaged in deconstructive wordplay as sophisticated as Derrida's as he connects the meanings of "the" and "thee," both words that pin something or someone in space—they are "shifters" because their referent constantly shifts. Just as the Nova Criminals shift coordinate points, this referent shifting demonstrates the instability of language, the slipperiness of any signifier. The article "the" strives to designate a specific person, place, or thing. Meanwhile the archaic second-person singular object pronoun "thee" wants to pin the individual down as a particular subject (or perhaps even an object since it is in the objective case). However, the word "the" functions in one final fashion in this passage: when it is capitalized to give "The Word"—*logos* or the master signifier. Control would have people believe in "The Word" like the various religions believe in infallibility of "The Word of God," but Hassan is demonstrating how such language usage controls people on a basic, almost imperceptible level: it labels humanity, defines humanity, and ensnares humanity in dual traps of time and the body while simultaneously demonstrating methods of attacking language: "The great skies are open" (2) to those who can relinquish language and the body, to free themselves from time and the alien virus of the word.

Burroughs's theories in the Nova trilogy are already pushing beyond the structuralist and into poststructural territory both in terms of language and power as well as the relation between the two. He is one of the first authors to explore how language structures and controls the subject, and his theories parallel or presage many others. As Lacan argued, the subject remains trapped between the signifiers that point toward it—they do not define it because, as Lacan argued, there is no signified. Burroughs made a similar argument in the cut-up novels, but he tied it directly into the power and control—Lacan did to an extent as well, but for him the repositories of power reside in the name of the father, the signifier itself, the psychoanalyst, and the academy. Control wants people to believe in the signified and its value—the subject needs the relation between signified and signifier, symbolized by the barre, the Lacanian psychoanalytical term for the line that simultaneously separates and joins the signifier and the signified in Ferdinand de Sausurre's semiotics. The barre connects signifiers to tangible objects and ideas, but both Burroughs and Lacan refuse the comfort of the barre by erasing it and the signified altogether. The media, the government, and various other institutions manipulate the signifier, usually to provide the subject with a master signifier, a signifier that provides a starting point for the signifying chain: this could be God, the Declaration of Independence, or the Big Bang. Each of them, whether factual or not, provides the subject with a stable narrative in which their character fits—the subject desires so much to be a meaningful character in the overall drama of existence. Lacan offered no real solution to the problem other than to describe the state of the human and the various responses that the human exhibits in response to it. The existentialists granted that existence had no inherent meaning—there was no inherent essence, that would require a master signifier. They also agreed with Lacan about the lack residing at the heart of the human condition, but they offered a solution: the subject can create its own meaning or essence. Influenced by existentialism Deleuze and Guattari (a philosopher and psychoanalyst, respectively) saw psychoanalysis as inherently dystopic because its ideal was functional neurosis (an absolute cure remains impossible according to the traditional school of psychoanalytical thought), and they sought a means of connecting the psychoanalytical with the liberatory strategies of Marxism. Collaborating with each other, they developed an alternative to psychoanalysis that they termed "schizoanalysis." According to schizoanalysis the lack within the human condition results from social, economic, and cultural forces. Schizoanalysis seeks to liberate subjects from socially inscribed neuroses, allowing them to define their own selves. Schizoanalysis proves more radical than existentialism because it creates a utopian goal for the subject, and, as Jameson says about utopias, they must be imagined and cast off repeatedly on the path toward revolution or liberation. The utopian goal is the to erase the desire that society has implanted in humans—buy, buy, buy; get a breast implant; earn millions; become an important figure in society; build the biggest house on the block; get as much pussy or cock as you can. Our company can show you the way—you are just four days away from being a millionaire with a fifteen-inch cock.

Burroughs went even further than all of them, and before Deleuze and Guattari developed their theories. He did write while Lacan was giving his lectures and refining his theories, but there is no evidence that he was aware of this work—he did harbor a virulent hatred for psychoanalysis, mostly because of his many years of sessions that he saw as fruitless. Burroughs took a different approach; his central idea resides in the basic statement: "Fuck them all. Squares on both sides" (*Naked Lunch* 16).

Following Hassan's monologue *Nova Express* presents an epistle from Inspector Lee that serves as a warning and a call to action. If a person is not resisting, then her or she is a collaborator. After espousing this false dichotomy, Lee explains that humanity has all been poisoned, that control (or the Nova Criminals) have monopolized every aspect of existence and bred subjects on false promises. The novel then leaps to a meta level as Lee mentions *Naked Lunch* and *The Soft Machine* as well as the book being read: "The purpose of my writing is to expose and arrest Nova Criminals. In *Naked Lunch The Soft Machine* and *Nova Express* I show who they are and what they are doing and what they will do if they are not arrested. Minutes to go. Souls rotten from their orgasm drugs, flesh shuddering from their nova ovens, prisoners of the earth *to come out*. With your help we can occupy The Reality Studio and retake their universe of Fear Death and Monopoly—" (5). *Naked Lunch* and the Nova trilogy serve as Lee-Burroughs's manifesto for identifying and then destroying the control machinery. The rest of the novel portrays a series of tales that play out against this background as the Nova Police and the Nova Criminals battle one another. As with the other cut-ups, Burroughs presented straightforward narrative at times and then cut it up and folded in other texts, always erasing his trail behind him just as Hassan i Sabbah canceled his own words.

The Job, the Cut-Up Films, and Other Experiments

Burroughs spent the bulk of the 1960s extending his cut-up experiments beyond the literary and into photography, film, and audio. *The Job* serves as the linchpin text for tying the whole *Naked Lunch* and cut-up period together. Ostensibly a series of interviews with David Odier, *The Job* actually features a series of essays that serve as Burroughs's manifesto on the cut-ups method and the power structure of control with interview sections peppered throughout the book. While *Minutes to Go* and *The Exterminator* explained the aesthetics, technique, and purpose of the cut-ups, they remained hard to find and obscure, and *The Third Mind* would not be published until the 1970s. Furthermore many of these texts' pronouncements are couched in experimental forms that make the ideas much muddier than the straightforward prose of *The Job*. In *The Job* Burroughs not only discussed the Nova novels but also espoused his worldview on a variety of topics. In many ways *The Job* acts as Burroughs's manifesto, his statement of purpose for both his life and his works.

Burroughs not only theorized the concepts in *The Job;* he put them into daily action with his experiments at the Beat Hotel. Along with Gysin and

Sommerville, Burroughs conducted audio experiments: recording audio, cutting it up, and folding in audio from other sources. He also produced what are generally referred to as "the cut-up scrapbooks," which feature Burroughs's own writing, other texts that he has pasted in, and photo collages. These experiments allowed Burroughs to practice his techniques on not just text as in the novels or the verbal as in the audio experiments but also the visuals. These notebooks provide a fascinating look into Burroughs's process during this period and feature writings in Burroughs's own script as well as images he has pasted in as in a scrapbook. Again all this work proved frustrating to Burroughs's publishers because he continued to pour out pages and pages of unpublishable material. Therefore most of these scrapbooks remain unpublished, but *The Burroughs File* includes a sampling of them that can provide the student with an idea of the work that Burroughs was conducting during this period. Essentially the scrapbooks show Burroughs honing his craft with the cut-ups and taking them as far as he could go until he exhausted the form. Only once he exhausted the aesthetic could he move on to new literary approaches, but there was one step beyond the combination of cut-up text and images. The next obvious step is film, which combines all the other forms into one; Burroughs achieved this goal by collaborating on a series of short films with Antony Balch. *The Cut-Ups, Towers Open Fire, Bill and Tony,* and *William Buys a Parrot* feature Burroughs in the films while also applying his cut-up approach. While Burroughs did not direct the films himself, he did collaborate, and they provide a glimpse of the possibilities of cut-ups in the cinematic medium. Burroughs also went on to adopt a filmic metaphor or structure for *The Wild Boys* and other subsequent works. Like the cut-ups this filmic metaphor became a permanent part of Burroughs's aesthetic lexicon because it too problematized the structure of language and images, as well as the genres produced within them.

The Last Words of Dutch Schultz does not fit neatly into the Cut-Up trilogy or the *Wild Boys* period because it blends the cut-up aesthetic with Burroughs's burgeoning interest in the camera eye as a means of narrative description. Timothy Murphy grouped it into Burroughs's middle period along with the wild boys novels and other texts; however, the novel and screenplay should really be considered as a mix of the old and new aesthetics. *The Last Words of Dutch Schultz* was written and published during the same period as *The Wild* Boys, and it demonstrates Burroughs's new fascination with a cinematic narrative style but still participates fully in the cut-up style. While *The Last Words of Dutch Schultz* proves interesting as a transitional piece, it also proves Burroughs's point that cut-ups exist within the natural world and that consciousness itself represents a cut-up as readers are bombarded with sensory perceptions, texts, images, and so on from all sides that must be processed. Similarly the book *The Last Words of Dutch Schultz*—labeling it as a screenplay or a novel proves extremely problematic—presents the reader with actual text from the gangster's already cut-up structure of his rambling last words, which Burroughs has rearranged in screenplay format including scene descriptions, director-cinematographer directions on mise-en-scène, and, of course, snippets of dialogue from Flegenheimer's fevered state. Alongside this surrealistic film script, the novel features numerous images of the notorious gangster, newspaper headlines from the period, and more. The book actually opens with an image of Dutch's corpse, setting a chillingly realistic aesthetic for the pages that follow. The book bends reality by taking the verisimilitude of photography and the Schultz transcript and then manipulating it into a kind of narrative or fiction. *The Last Words of Dutch Schultz* breaks down the line between reality and fiction and depicts reality as a film, like in the Cut-Up trilogy, a reality that is ultimately written by the agents of control. Here Burroughs himself took on the role of control agent by controlling the reader's perceptions of reality and history.

Like Joyce's *Finnegans Wake,* Beckett's trilogy, or the French experiments with the *nouveau roman,* the cut-ups lead ultimately to an exhaustion of the literary. At a certain point, they could not be pushed any further. Hence Burroughs holstered them as a tool to be utilized at strategic moments in his later writings but as a technique that had reached a kind of experimental cul-de-sac and so could no longer provide Burroughs's only form, not if he were to continue to push his writing into new territories. Cut-ups might remain useful, but new forms had to be sought if Burroughs's continued evolution as a writer, like the evolution of humankind that he so ardently desired, depended on sloughing off one skin to grow a new, larger one that progresses ever more toward the full, mature form. While Burroughs quit producing material that was mostly cut-up, he never abandoned the technique—it reappears throughout his later works to one degree or another to always scramble what Burroughs had already written to constantly remind the reader that all language, even Burroughs's, remains compromised and cannot be trusted because it can always be interpreted in any number of different ways.

CHAPTER 5

Rainbow Jockstraps and Death Gods

The Nomadic War Machine in *The Wild Boys* Period

In the 1970s, Burroughs moved away from extreme experimentalism and returned to penning fiction with more linear narratives, the most important of which were the "Wild Boys" novels. In many ways, the "Wild Boys Tetralogy," as some Burroughs critics have labeled it, serves as a transitional series of works between the 1960s Nova trilogy and the Red Night trilogy of the 1980s. Themes, style, and imagery from the 1960s still linger, but Burroughs also began exploring the themes of his later trilogy. The novel *The Wild Boys* served as the inspiration for David Bowie's classic Ziggy Stardust persona, and the titular characters provide the inspiration for the eponymous Duran Duran song of the 1980s. *The Wild Boys* introduced a series of four loosely connected novels in which Burroughs began to increasingly focus on revolutionary groups who attacked from the margins, a theme that would reach maturation in his Red Night trilogy. Focusing on gay adolescent revolutionaries, *The Wild Boys: A Book of the Dead* unfolds as a film presented to the reader in novelistic form, and the iconic look of the novel's characters profoundly influenced dystopian science fiction, particularly postapocalyptic sci-fi in the 1980s. Aside from its fascinating group of protagonists, the novel also continues Burroughs's investigations into power, control, and revolt. In these works Burroughs further refined his conceptualization of control as a force that can be subverted and turned against itself through the creation of alternate (abject) spaces. Burroughs continued these explorations in the short story anthology *Exterminator!* (1973), the time-travel novel *Port of Saints* (1973), and the graphic novel *Ah Pook Is Here*. *Ah Pook Is Here* proves particularly interesting because it was intended to be a graphic novel collaboration with artist Malcolm McNeill; however, a lack of funding left the project in limbo. A mostly text version appeared in 1979, but McNeill's complete illustrations were not finally released until 2012. The wild boys novels show Burroughs continuing to hone his theories of control and beginning to explore how time and space relate to power.

In these works Burroughs moved from the dystopian visions of his previous works to an interest in the possibility of utopia. *The Wild Boys* still maintains many of Burroughs's earlier themes but transports them into a chaotic landscape populated by revolutionary bands of "wild boys," teenage boys who have rejected society's control in favor of absolute freedom. As some contend, *Port of Saints* is basically just *The Wild Boys II* because it continues the story of the wild boys, as their ideology (or lack of one) begins to spread virally into a global phenomenon. The virus metaphor that has always been present in Burroughs's writing now becomes a methodology of utopian praxis. No doubt some of Burroughs's interest in utopias stemmed from his constant interest in Hassan i Sabbah, master of assassins, and his mountain fortress called Alamut. Burroughs explained that Hassan i Sabbah was a member of "the dissident Ishmaelian sect" of Islam, who created a base of operations "in the mountain fortress of Alamut in what is now northern Iran (*The Book of Breeething* 102). Alamut became an "all male community of several hundred apprentice assassins," a community in which Burroughs believed that "undoubtedly homosexual practices formed a part of the training" (102). Whether this ancient Islamic assassin organization engaged in homosexual practices or whether it is merely a phantasmatic (or even masturbatory) projection on Burroughs's part remains an object of speculation. Nevertheless Hassan i Sabbah, whose presence proved crucial in the Nova trilogy, still looms large in the wild boys books as Burroughs begins to conceive of a gendered utopia. Once again this brings up the question of Burroughs's alleged misogyny, but he maintained that the splitting of the human species into male and female provided one of the major roadblocks for future human evolution. Therefore an all-male, all-homosexual society would open the door to new evolutionary potentials if the problem of propagation could be solved.

The Camera Eye: Visibility and Utopia in *The Wild Boys* and *Port of Saints*

Port of Saints continues the tale of the wild boys, so the two should be considered together. *The Wild Boys* features the subtitle *A Book of Dead*, seemingly placing it in the tradition of the Egyptian and Tibetan books of the dead, which provide instructions for the afterlife. Burroughs always claimed that all the characters in *The Wild Boys* are dead. The wild boys themselves constitute a new kind of revolutionary group: roving, nomadic bands of homosexual males. Their age is debatable as is often the case when Burroughs mentions "boys," but one can assume that they are somewhere between adolescence and adulthood. The boys remain innocent in a way and still capable of transformation—they have not been as firmly locked in the control machine as older adults who have experienced more time to internalize control. They are not a clean slate (a tabula rasa as John Locke would term the natural human state, or a plane of immanence or body without organs as Deleuze would term it), but the organizational structures within these subjects remain fewer and more permeable, more open to subversion. As Nietzsche famously stated, "One must still have chaos in one's soul if one is to give birth to a dancing star." The emphasis here relies on chaos and the manner of utopian thought as flawed—like Marx and Engels's vision of a communist utopia—however, the would-be revolutionary (or utopian) must embrace chaos and this possibility of failure. Only with the willingness to reject current organizational structures as elements of control can the subject transform him- or herself into the abject by submitting to chaos and the flows within it. They must embrace the chaos of a nomadic existence and sexual lifestyle with no rules (other than the exclusion of women). Like Peter Pan and the Lost Boys, they refuse the social ideals of proper aging to remain free. Because they remain free, they tap into the theories of control and revolution that Deleuze, Guattari, and de Certeau discussed in their various works. Despite its apocalyptic setting, which Jimmy Fazzino maintained is not necessarily a bad thing for Burroughs, the wild boy's tales bring Burroughs's work and revolutionary theory out of the abstract concepts of the cut-ups and down to street level where not just subversion but utopia becomes a possibility even if that utopia remains a the roving one of the nomadic children and teenagers.

The Wild Boys features the aesthetic of a film with the scenes being described as shots. Burroughs always claimed that the "Camera Eye" sections that appear throughout John Dos Passos's U.S.A. trilogy (*The 42nd Parallel, 1919,* and *The Big Money*) were a major inspiration for the cut-ups because of their fractured viewpoint: the camera of Dos Passos's trilogy flits around wildly catching brief images of the United States of the period. The camera eye was a twist on the modernist fascination with stream of consciousness. Dos Passos tapped into the emerging medium of film and combined it with the stream of consciousness technique to demonstrate not how technology was beginning to alter the nature of perception. *The Wild Boys* signaled Burroughs's move away from cut-ups and features little of the technique; however, the cut-up method will continue appear in snippets throughout Burroughs's fiction. Burroughs's use of the film metaphor in *The Wild Boys* is not random or cut-up—it uses screenplay directions to establish shots, marking the story as a memoir of the dead. Burroughs continued to use film stylings in other works such as *The Last Words of Dutch Shultz* and *Blade Runner: A Movie.*

Douglas Baldwin traced what he called "Burroughs's bipolar response" to film throughout his oeuvre and argued that Burroughs felt "on the one hand, a fascination with narrative methodologies developed along with the growth of the various technologies of the moving image as they suggest potential 'cinematic storytelling' that he could imitate in language, and, on the other hand, an increasing suspicion of the potential social 'control' technologies of the moving image may have over the individual" (64). The film metaphor plays out most explicitly in the Penny Arcade Peep Show sections that appear throughout the novel—these tie the story back into the early days of film and machines such as the kinetoscope, which allowed viewers to insert coins to view short films. It is important to note that pornographic films have existed since the beginning of cinema. The medium has always been voyeuristic, and Burroughs connected these sections directly to that proclivity. Indeed control functions as the quintessential voyeur since its goal is to observe and consequently direct subject behavior. This has only become truer in an era when someone or something is always filming. Again control has willingly been accepted by citizens who now constantly serve as spies and collaborators without even knowing it.

Burroughs's new aesthetic did not drastically change the content of the novel: he still presented the reader with scenes of graphic sex, violence, and mutation. The wild boys wage war against those who would try to squash their group—a marginally free group poses a serious threat to the system of control. Control must either eliminate these abject individuals or reappropriate them into society—they must either be interpellated into subjects or exterminated en masse. The wild boys manage to successfully fend off most attacks from the agents of control, but one problem persists. To remain a viable revolutionary group, they must be able to expand their ranks. Today this might be achieved via social media as has been the case with ISIS, men's rights advocates, and the alt-right; however, this technology does not exist in the novel. More and more boys run off to join the group, but the wild boys cannot rely on this method of recruitment—they must breed wild boys. Therefore they must devise a means to appropriate the machinery of reproduction for themselves.

The characters in *Port of Saints* attempt to learn to reproduce without the aid of women. They experiment with cloning, which will become the homosexual male characters' means of dismissing women from their society: "our laboratories were working round the clock on the clone project, but we were still dependent on the border cities for male babies, where a semen and baby black market flourished despite periodic crackdowns. You could take your boyfriend's semen to town, line up fifty Arab girls and take the male crop back to your village" (91). Later, using sex magic, the wild boys attain a level of complete independence from the female: "Here are the boys cooking over campfires quiet valley by a mountain stream. They have stepped back into the dawn before creation. No female was ever made from the flesh that turns to yellow light in the rising sun. The phallic gods of Greece, the assassins of Alamut and the Old Man himself, dispossessed by generations of female conquest. . . . We will show you the sex magic that turns flesh to light. We will free you forever from the womb" (93–94). Once they are "freed from the womb," then they can truly begin to expand their society. They will solve what Burroughs saw as the insoluble conflict that bars human evolution—the division of the species into two sexes.

The wild boys mythology and the issues with which it dealt are expanded on in *Exterminator!* and *Ah Pook Is Here,* texts that do not fit neatly into a tetralogy because there is no direct continuation of story but that are generally grouped with the two novels because of the recurring characters and themes. Virus B-23 makes its first appearance in *Exterminator!,* the second novel to include stories of the wild boys. The number 23 appears throughout the novel as a running motif, but the virus makes its appearance only halfway through the novel in the section entitled "What Washington? What Orders?" Even in this early incarnation, Virus B-23 proves to be a violent mutation of the "word," and the "word" becomes the primary evolutionary advancement of mankind, an advancement that is as detrimental as it is stupendous: "The word that made a man out of an ape and killed the ape in the process keeps man an animal the way we like to see him. And the Queen is just another prop to hold up the word. You all know what we can do with the word. Talk about the power in an atom. All hate all fear all pain all death all sex is in the word. The word was a killer virus once. It could become a killer again. The word is too hot to handle so we sit on our ass waiting for the pension. But somebody is going to pick up that virus and use it . . . *Virus B-23*" (*Exterminator!* 114). This passage hearkens back to the last chapter of *The Soft Machine,* in which Burroughs depicted the evolutionary step of humans crawling out of the mud with the talk sickness. Thus for Burroughs the word remains a virus, one that must be "exterminated," as the novel's title indicates, if further evolution is to be achieved.

Ah Pook Is Here has complicated history because it started as a graphic novel project with Burroughs providing the text and British artist Malcolm McNeill providing the elaborate full-color illustrations of the story. Malcolm McNeill recalled the long road of trying to publish *Ah Pook Is Here,* a road that ultimately ended in failure. The color illustrations proved too costly to publish at the time. To drum up interest in the graphic novel, Burroughs published a volume entitled *Ah Pook Is Here and Other Texts,* a volume featuring the *Ah Pook Is Here* story or novella (depending on definition) as well as *The Book of Breeething* and *The Electronic Revolution,* both of which were published as separate works. Out of print for many years, *Ah Pook Is Here and Other Texts* remains the only published version of the story although audio recordings of Burroughs's reading of it are readily available. One major issue surrounding any current attempt to critically read *Ah Pook Is Here* resides in the problematic publication of the text. The compromised, published version features some black-and-white illustrations, but now there also is Malcolm McNeil's artwork for the graphic novel that *Ah Pook* was supposed to become. Burroughs's story of *Ah Pook* proves rather simplistic, but McNeill's images depict a tale of revolutionaries, societies broken down in orgiastic chaos, and so on. Some of McNeill's images remain sketches and almost never feature the words for the speech and thought balloons. Thus the current scholar is faced with the problem that not all the images can be easily correlated to Burroughs's story—they seem to hint toward a much grander vision.

Ah Pook concerns Mr. Hart and his quest for immortality via the Mayan codices, but the story also features what is now "Control" in its most literal form. Mr. Hart seeks control not only over life and the living but also over death. He even orders that the word "death" not be spoken on his premises. Hart's quest is not so different from Burroughs's theoretical direction, except that Burroughs seeks freedom while Hart seeks control. Mr. Hart provides the *anthropomorphization* of control in this book, and his desire stretches beyond control of the living—he desires to control the afterlife as well, to control the gods. Mr. Hart demonstrates how control always seeks to lengthen its grasp, to more perfectly control not just individuals but the physical world as well. This becomes especially apparent during the section of the novel in which the narrator visits a computer called Control, which proves apropos since Deleuze argued that the computer serves as the paradigmatic technology of the control age. The question is posed: "Is Control controlled by its need to Control?" The computer responds in the affirmative, and this is how control functions. If a certain section of society resists control, such as the wild boys, then it must be either assimilated or annihilated. If a certain class of humans or sector of society can be controlled more perfectly, then control must perfect its machinery. However, Mr. Hart seeks more—he seeks to spread Control beyond this world and into the next one. The Control computer also ties Control into time. The interlocutor asks Control, "If Control's control is absolute why does control need to control?" Control responds simply that "Control needs time." The narrator explains, "Exactly control needs time in which to exercise control just as

DEATH needs time to kill. If DEATH killed everyone at birth or Control installed electrodes in their brains at birth there would be no time left in which to kill or control" (31).

Taking It to the Streets: Ancillary Texts from the 1970s

The published book *Ah Pook Is Here and Other Texts* also features two additional texts: *The Book of Breeething* and *The Electronic Revolution,* both of which were published as independent books in small editions and deserve discussion in their own right. *The Electronic Revolution* also appears as the concluding essay in *The Job*—its depiction of enacting revolutionary practices in the real world generates an ideal segue into a discussion of Burroughs's "Red Night" novels. Finally another small publication, the illustrated work *The Four Horsemen of the Apocalypse,* provides a final discussion of communication, control, and revolution that will provide the last components of Burroughs's overall project and philosophy before the penning of the "Red Night" novels, which many consider to be not just his final major works but also his magnum opus, a culmination of his life's work.

Written some years later, *Blade Runner: A Movie* took Burroughs's interest in film into new territory. The novella's title has an interesting history. Burroughs took the title and some inspiration for his novel from Alan Nourse's science fiction novel *The Bladerunner,* and Burroughs received permission from Nourse to use the title. Of course the title became famous only with the release of Ridley Scott's film *Blade Runner,* a neonoir and cyberpunk adaptation of Philip K. Dick's classic novel *Do Androids Dream of Electric Sheep?,* which shares no similarities with Nourse's or Burroughs's novels other than the title.

Blade Runner opens as a movie pitch and then proceeds into a scene-by-scene description of the film's contents without ever turning into a screenplay. The novel starts with this pitch to B.J., a callback to the opening section of *The Ticket That Exploded:* "See the Action, B.J.?" The name "B.J." recalls bigshot Hollywood, but, of course, it also signifies a blow job, thus illustrating Burroughs's continual recycling of earlier material and his constant need to create sexual double entendres. The hopeful scriptwriter describes a future in which the FDA and AMA achieve even more influence over the lives of American citizens: "This film is about overpopulation and the growth of vast service bureaucracies. The FDA and AMA and the big drug companies are like an octopus on the citizen. You're dying of cancer, see? The doctor gives you no hope, wants you out of his office as quick as possible because you don't carry health insurance or qualify for Medicare" (2). Instead the doctor merely offers the patient painkillers. Meanwhile there are numerous alternative forms of treatment that have been blocked by the FDA, partly because they receive payouts from pharmaceutical industry lobbyists, who want to keep the options as slim as possible and the prices as high as possible.

Virus B-23 makes another early appearance in *Blade Runner,* but here it is a form of cancer: "The film is about cancer and that's a powerful project. Already doctors are talking about an epidemic. In the film a strain of epidemic flash cancer is stopped by virus B-23, a virus of biological mutation, a virus of biologic mutation which restores humanity to pristine health" (4). A virus that can cure humans could prove very detrimental to upper-class doctors, insurance companies, and politicians who receive donations from lobbyists because it would erase the necessity of their services; however, at present, the regulation of medicine remains controlled by the governments and corporations. Otherwise one must turn to the blossoming black market. As the speaker explains, "This is the background against which the film revolves. Any treatment, any drug, and vice can be found here for a price" (n.p.). Overpopulation has led to the growth of control, and *Blade Runner* provides a very concise definition of control: "Overpopulation has led to ever-increasing governmental control over the private citizen, not on the old-style police-state models of oppression and terror, but in terms of work, credit, housing, retirement benefits, and medical-care: services that can be withheld. These services are computerized. No number, no service." To escape the grasp of control, many individuals have chosen to relinquish their subjecthood and become abject—the numberless individuals who live in the underground.

The government was under pressure to pass a health care act, but it was universally opposed by doctors, insurance companies, and individuals who did not want to pay "to keep the niggers and the spics and the beatniks in hotels and hospitals" (n.p.). This situation almost directly parallels the situation in the United States except that, in the novel, the refusal to pass a health care bill led to the Health Care Riots of 1984. The subsequent Firearms Registration Act barred almost everyone who was not middle class or above from owning any type of firearm, thus forestalling any future revolts. With people robbed of their ability to revolt and lacking a government that provides for them, a large medical black market develops. The blade runners serve an essential function because they transfer drugs and medical equipment between providers, underground doctors, and clients. These doctors require blade runners because it is a felony for doctors to possess unlicensed medical supplies but only a misdemeanor for other citizens. *Blade Runner* demonstrates how totalitarianism is no longer necessary for Control to function. Normal legal channels can be used to ever more perfectly control the populace.

CHAPTER 6

Out of Time and into Space

Humanity's Evolutionary Potential in the "Red Night" Novels

Unlike the Wild Boys books of the 1970s, the Red Night trilogy offers a more radical and organized system of utopian revolution. While the novels constitute another major shift in Burroughs's writing, they also represent a culmination of all his previous works into one final vision. Old Burroughs characters and phrases are recycled, and he has returned to all the genres he has used before: science fiction, hard-boiled crime, surrealist body horror, and so on. The depiction of utopia shifts as well as *Cities of the Red Night* moves on to *The Western Lands. Cities of the Red Night* expands on his utopian ideals of nomadic war machines because Burroughs knew this is not enough—these utopian cadres remain trapped in time. To shatter these temporal chains, humankind must look beyond to a space of pure immanence. Therefore as readers progress from the *Cities of the Red Night* to *The Western Lands,* they experience different utopian ideals and failures, various depictions of revolution and social collapse, and the constant struggle between control and radical freedom. The forces of control have stalled the process of natural selection, mutation, and evolution—they have bred humankind into a cul-de-sac. The control society, as Deleuze explained, creates "dividuals," but the Red Night trilogy demonstrates how humankind can recapture their individuality. Of course these final revelations are not revealed until *The Western Lands,* so they must be set aside for a moment to consider the first two novels in the trilogy.

Michel de Certeau's concept of "tactics" and "strategies" helps to demarcate the utopian ideas that separate *The Wild Boys* from *Cities of the Red Night.*

In *The Practice of Everyday Life,* he defined two types of possible forms of action in the postmodern world: tactics and strategies. De Certeau used the term "strategy" to refer to "the calculus of force relationships which becomes possible when a subject of will and power . . . can be isolated from an environment. A strategy assumes a place that can be circumscribed as proper (*propre*) and thus serve as the basis for generating relations with an exterior distinct from it" (de Certeau xix). A "tactic," on the other hand, is defined as "a calculus which cannot count on a 'proper' (a spatial or institutional localization), nor thus on a borderline distinguishing the other as a visible totality" (xix). The tactic "has at its disposal no base where it can capitalize on its advantages, prepare its expansions, and secure independence with respect to circumstances. The 'proper' is a triumph of place over time. On the contrary, because it does not have a place, a tactic depends on time—it is always on the watch for opportunities that must be seized 'on the wing.' Whatever it wins, it does not keep" (37).

The Red Night revolutionaries want to move beyond the tactics of the wild boys, which were still subject to time and hence control. As de Certeau pointed out, the strategy constitutes a "victory of space over time" (37), which had been Burroughs's project since the cut-outs. However, it is only in the Red Night trilogy that he realizes what has been missing—a proper. The abject have always relied on tactics because they were marginalized and incapable of seizing spaces of their own. The wild boys took tactics to their limit by organizing abject individuals into groups, nomadic war machines as Deleuze would term them, but nomadic groups can hold spaces, so strategies become necessary to seize spaces that can themselves be rendered as abject.

Pirate Utopias and Sex Viruses: *Cities of the Red Night*

The first novel of the trilogy, *Cities of the Red Night,* heralds a return to narrative clarity that had been absent from Burroughs's writing since his first two novels—*Junky* and *Queer.* The novel opens with a historical account of a liberal utopian pirate commune founded by the pirate Captain Mission in the eighteenth century. Captain Mission founded the colony of Libertatia, which was governed by a set of articles that "state[d], among other things: all decisions with regard to the colony [are] to be submitted to vote by the colonists; the abolition of slavery for any reason including debt; the abolition of the death penalty; and freedom to follow any religious beliefs or practices without sanction or molestation" (xii). The historical account of Captain Mission parallels almost exactly the story of Captain Strobe's pirate commune, Port Roger, in the novel, and it displays Burroughs's new utopian ideals of revolution: the abject must band together and create zones from which to strike.

Burroughs divided the structure of *Cities of the Red Night* into alternating chapters dealing with three major stories: the story of Virus B-23 that originated in the six ancient Cities of the Red Night and was rediscovered in 1923, the story of Noah Blake's adventures with the pirate revolutionary named Captain Strobe, and the first-person narrative of private detective Clem Snide, who turns out to be the grand writer of all three distinct stories as they become interrelated at the novel's end. Burroughs opened the novel in 1923 with the outbreak of Virus B-23 in the city of Waghdas, one of the ancient Cities of the Red Night, but the story promptly whisks the reader back in time through a picture entitled "The Hanging of Captain Strobe the Gentleman Pirate. Panama City, May 13, 1702" (27). Burroughs again has used filmic language to narrate the event: "A Sepia Etching onscreen . . . the etching comes alive, giving off a damp heat, a smell of weeds and mud flats and sewage" (27). Soon the reader becomes a part of the "silent . . . waiting" crowd that watches Strobe's hanging as the tale of Noah Blake is related (27).

Noah Blake and his five friends enlist to sail out of their home in Harbor Point on a ship called *The Great-White,* which is captained by a man named Opium Jones. The novel, then, shifts to a first-person account, and Noah is allowed to narrate his own story. Through the journal entries of Noah Blake, the reader learns of his struggles with repression and discrimination in his hometown:

> From earliest memory I have felt myself a stranger in the village of Harbor Point where I was born. Who was I? . . . And who are the others—Brady, Hansen, Paco, Todd? Strangers like myself. I think that we came from another world and have been stranded here like mariners on some barren and hostile shore. I never felt that what we did together was wrong, but I fully understood the necessity and wisdom of concealing it from the villagers. Now that there is no need for concealment, I feel as if this ship is the home I had left and thought never to find again. (60–61)

Noah's feelings of liberation presage the life he will discover in the utopian commune of Port Roger, which, like Captain Mission's Libertatia, seeks to free people from the shackles of racial, religious, and (in Burroughs's version) sexual discrimination; that is, to free them from their interpellation into subjects and to allow their abjectivity to prosper.

Captain Strobe's pirates capture *The Great-White,* leading to Noah's arrival at Port Roger, which causes Noah to imagine the landing scene as a painting, obviously reminiscent of the painting that introduced the story of Strobe: "I had the curious impression of looking at a painting in a gold frame: the two ships riding at anchor in the still blue harbor, a cool morning breeze, and written on the bottom of the frame: 'Port Roger—April 1, 1702.' This day presents itself to my memory as a series of paintings" (93). Noah narrates the remainder of the chapter as a series of paintings entitled *The Oarsmen, Unloading the Cargo, Radiant Boys,* and *Captain Nordenholz Disembarks at Port Roger* (93–96). Port Roger itself proves to be little more than a painting disguised as just another section of the jungle, for, after their trek through the jungle, their trail "ends in a screen of bamboo"; however, Noah notices that "the bamboo trees are painted on a green door that swings open like the magic door in a book" (97). Thus Port Roger lies concealed from outside gazes by appearing to be part of the surrounding jungle. Strobe's pirates have also painted the interior of the town in order to make it blend with the jungle. They have demarcated Port Roger as their "proper" and concealed it from the exterior gaze of the control apparatus through this strategy, which features their attempt at creating a space where their abjectivity can flourish.

Skipper Nordenholz explains that the group's major enemy is Spain and that their main weapon "is the freedom hope of captive peoples now enslaved and peonized under the Spanish" (103). The pirates of Port Roger seek allies in all the alienated and oppressed peoples of the world, a mission similar in many respects to Captain Mission's Libertatia, which found its "allies in all those who are enslaved and oppressed throughout the world" (xiii). While their main interest is the Spanish, who are the primary source of control in South American area near Port Roger, the revolutionaries are concerned with breaking the control lines that enslave all the various peoples of the world. Therefore just as the Nova Police sought allies in criminals, the pirates will free oppressed people in order to also grow their ranks and potentially create liberated sites that could act as new propers.

While the Port Roger pirates do not operate through the beastly means of the wild boys, they have even more dangerous weapons, weapons reminiscent of those that the forces of control would employ. Dr. Benway reappears with a plan for using illness as a weapon while the Iguana Girl plans to use magical weaponry against the "Christian monopoly" (105). The Iguana Girl explains how this "Christian monopoly" has effectively created a series of abject groups that can easily be united and brought over to the side of the Port Roger pirates: "All religions are magical systems competing with other systems. The Church has driven magic into covens where practitioners are bound to each other by a common fear. We can unite the Americas into a vast coven of those who live under the Articles, united against the Christian Church. Catholic and Protestant. It is our policy to encourage the practice of magic and to introduce alternative religious beliefs to break the Christian monopoly" (105). Religion, like other forces of control, creates potential revolutionary groups through its restrictive laws. These laws themselves attempt to govern all aspects of life (and the afterlife), and they further create subaltern groups just waiting for a leader to organize them into a revolutionary army; Strobe and his followers hope to be such leaders.

The Iguana Girl is one of those surprisingly positive female characters that are rare—but that do sporadically appear—in Burroughs's writings, particularly in the Red Night trilogy. Another such female character appears at the end of the chapter, and the reader glimpses Burroughs, for just a few seconds, narrating through the voice of a woman—Hirondelle de Mer. Together these two female characters help to illuminate the role of women in Port Roger; after all if a community is to function then it must have the capacity for reproduction, and if a society desires to pass as normal, then women prove necessary. For the revolution to be successful, settlements such as Port Roger must be created across the globe, and, as Nordenholz explains, for this to be successful, the revolutionaries need families to bolster their cause:

> We have already established fortified settlements . . . as you see, practically unlimited. We need artisans, soldiers, sailors, and farmers to man the settlements already founded and to establish new centers from the Bering Strait to the Cape. Breeding is encouraged . . . is in fact a duty, I hope not too unpleasant. We expect that some of you will raise families. In any case, mothers and children . . . well cared for, you understand. We need families to operate as intelligence agents in areas controlled by the enemy. (106)

Traditional, heterosexual family units are essential for Port Roger to appear like an ordinary town, and such families can also be used to infiltrate enemy areas as spies. Nordenholz then proceeds to introduce the "young ladies" with whom the men of Port Roger are expected to breed. After the women have lined up along one wall, the men line up along the opposite wall facing them, at which point Juanito, "the joker and Master of Ceremonies," says, "And now we will separate *los maridos,* the husbands, from *los hombres conejos,* the rabbit men, who fuck . . . and run" (106). Thus the men of Port Roger are split into two groups: the heterosexual men, who desire to take a wife and have a family; and the homosexual men, who will impregnate the women solely because of their sense of duty to Port Roger and who, as such, "fuck and run." What follows is a hilarious scene in which "the rabbit men," who apparently far outnumber "the husbands," group themselves together. Once the division has taken place, "the wives and husbands pair off and retire to private rooms," never to be mentioned again, since it is obvious that "the rabbit men" are not only the focus of the novel, but also the primary driving force behind the Port Roger revolutionaries (107).

"The rabbit men," who view women with feelings of utter disgust, enact a series of tableaux-like performances, which enable them to have intercourse with other men while impregnating the women. Then, astoundingly, Burroughs allows one of these women to speak for herself. While she does take part in the demeaning breeding rituals of Port Roger, Hirondelle de Mer seems to be an object of sympathy when she laments: "I am a sorceress and a warrior. I do not relish being treated as a breeding animal. Would this occur to Skipper Nordenholz? No force, he says, has been applied—but I am forced to by circumstances, cast up here without a peso, and by my Indian blood which compels me to side with all enemies of Spain. The child will be brought up a sorcerer or a sorceress" (111). Hirondelle de Mer even dreams of taking part in the revolution that Strobe, Nordenholz, and the others are fomenting: "They can only plan to hold the area by sorcery. This is a sorcerers' revolution. I must find my part as a sorceress" (112). Timothy S. Murphy claimed that the breeding with the women at Port Roger is "describing, for the first time in affirmative terms, heterosexual intercourse" (*Wising Up the Marks* 183). Coupled with the account of Hirondelle de Mer, this "demonstrate[s], for the first time in Burroughs's writing, that the sexes are not destined to be at war with each other but can form alliances against a common enemy" (184).

Aside from Hirondelle de Mer, the novel persistently casts women in villainous roles. For example early in the novel, during the discovery of Virus B-23 in modern times, Dr. Pierson reveals that the virus itself stems from the division between male and female. As usual Burroughs here has revealed women to be the bane of humankind's existence. Dr. Pierson equates the symptoms of Virus B-23—"fever, rash, a characteristic odor, sexual frenzies, obsession with sex and death"—with the effects of being in love: "Are not the symptoms of Virus B-23 simply the symptoms of what we are so pleased to call 'love'? Eve, we are told, was made from Adam's rib . . . so a hepatitis virus was once a healthy liver cell. If you will excuse me, ladies, nothing personal . . . we are all tainted with viral origins. The whole quality of human consciousness, as expressed in male and female, is basically a viral mechanism. I suggest that this virus, known as 'the other half,' turned malignant as a result of the radiation to which the Cities of the Red Night were exposed" (25). Thus the "Other Half" virus from the Cut-Up trilogy reappears in *Cities,* and characteristically Burroughs revealed women to be one of the primary sources of humankind's woes.

The Red Night, "when the whole northern sky lit up red at night," caused a variety of mutations, including, as Dr. Pierson points out, the mutation that spawns Virus B-23 (155). Soon "the mutants began to outnumber the original inhabitants, who were as all human beings were at the time: black" (155). Immediately following this catastrophic event, the women of Yass-Waddah revolted, and "led by an albino mutant known as the White Tigress, seized Yass-Waddah, reducing all the male inhabitants to slaves, consorts, and courtiers all under sentence of death that could be carried out at any time at the caprice of the White Tigress" (155–56). Later the reader discovers that "Yass-Waddah, a spaceport in rivalry with Ba'dan, is a matriarchy ruled by a hereditary empress" where men are mere "second-class citizens" (283). This rivalry culminates in a full-scale war between the cities and sexes. To prevent the destruction of Tamaghis and the blockading of Waghdas, the university city from which all knowledge is derived, the men of the other cities "foment" riots as "a prelude to an all-out assault on Yass-Waddah" (284). Their final objective is nothing less than the total eradication of Yass-Waddah. The male characters of the novel must not only destroy the city but also erase any memories that could prove that a matriarchal society could have ever wielded so much power. Like the pirates of Port Roger, the women of Yass-Waddah create their own "proper" by seizing control of the city and relegating the men to subservient positions. Thus the women have appropriated power and its mechanisms of control; however, they have consequently rendered one class as superior, and they have raised themselves to the subject position while relegating men to the abject. Despite some of its misogynistic flaws, Port Roger tries to improve on Yass-Waddah's model by accepting all different forms of oppressed people from both sexes and all manner of sexualities.

Destroying the Universe in *The Place of Dead Roads*

The trilogy's second novel, *The Place of Dead Roads,* features a different brand of utopian revolutionaries—a group of homosexual cowboys who seek liberation from the Puritanical forces surrounding them. The Johnsons, as they are called, like the Port Roger pirates, also seek to create a "proper" in Johnsonville from which they can lash out against the control machinery surrounding them. Early in his lifetime, Burroughs came across the idea of the Johnson family in Jack Black's novel *You Can't Win* (1926). The Johnsons from Black's novel provide the basis for Burroughs's utopian visions in *Dead Roads*. Burroughs's foreword to Black's *You Can't Win* provides a brief description of what it means to be a Johnson: "A Johnson pays his debts and keeps his word. He minds his own business, but will give help when help is needed and asked for. He does not hold out on his confederates or cheat his landlady. He is what they call in show business 'good people'" (11). The Johnsons represent a new form of revolutionary community, an almost communistic social order. The Johnsons' revolutionary agenda seeks to dismantle capitalistic ideology.

Kim Carsons, the central character of the novel, explains the communistic aspects of the Johnson Family when he states, "The Johnson Family is a cooperative structure. There isn't any boss man. People know what they are supposed to do and they do it. We're all actors and we change roles. Today's millionaire may be tomorrow's busboy. There's none of that ruling class old school tie" (114–15). Kim's comments are almost directly in line with the dream of annihilating class-based hierarchies from Marx and Engels's *Communist Manifesto* (1848): By doing away with class demarcations, the Johnsons create what can be termed a worker's utopia, a communistic reordering of society of which Marx and Engels would be proud. The Johnsons, thus, "represent a society of decentered, nonhierarchical socialist democracies with a communal economic base in agriculture and useful industry" (223). Through this creation of a cooperative social structure, the Johnsons hope to escape from these "common forms" and "general ideas" that have repeatedly oppressed them and forced them into conforming to the hegemonic, Aristotelian categories of Western civilization.

Kim Carsons, like Burroughs and Noah Blake, endured prejudice and discrimination as a young adolescent. Kim's interests as a young male radically differ from what would be considered appropriate in the nineteenth-century American west: "Kim is a slimy, morbid youth of unwholesome proclivities with an insatiable appetite for the extreme and the sensational. . . . Kim adores ectoplasms, crystal balls, spirit guides, and auras. He wallows in abominations, unspeakable rites, diseased demon lovers, loathsome secrets imparted in thick slimy whisper, ancient ruined cities under a purple sky, the smell of unknown excrements, the musky sweet rotten reek of the terrible Red Fever" (16).

Kim's studies thus tie the novel back into *Cities,* and his interests also parallel those of Burroughs as an outcast youth: "Kim is everything a normal American boy is taught to *detest*" (16). Not only does Kim indulge in hideous pastimes, but "he was also given to the subversive practice of *thinking,*" and he is "in fact incurably intelligent" (16). Kim, unlike Burroughs and Noah, experiences prejudice because of his cognitive capacity and nontraditional ideas instead of his sexuality: "Now American boys are told they should think. But just wait until your thinking is basically different from the thinking of a boss or a teacher. . . . You will find out that you aren't supposed to think" (16). Finding himself hated by traditional society, Kim begins to be fascinated by the legends of Hassan i Sabbah and his army of assassins: "How he longed to be a dedicated assassin in an all-male society" (20). Kim, of course, achieves his dream later in the novel when he founds Johnsonville, a society that does not discriminate based on independent and creative thought.

However, there are those within the capitalist order that want to see the Johnson movement squashed at all costs. "The evil old men who run America," Mr. Bickford and Mr. Hart—familiar by now from *Ah Pook*—hated "to see wealth and power in the hands of those who basically despised the usages of wealth and power" (104). As the Johnsons grow in power, they inevitably incite the anger of Mr. Hart and Mr. Bickford, who consequently send Colonel Greenfield to kill the Wild Fruits gang, Kim's own posse of Johnsons, which has been wreaking havoc on the capitalist social order in the Old West. However, when Greenfield finally catches up with the Wild Fruits, they are already dead from a mass suicide. With the help of cloning, Kim and his gang are reborn and populate the rest of the book in clone incarnations. Kim knows that to survive he must be subtler this time around; thus he decides to create communities that "pass" as normal towns to the Harts and Bickfords of the world but that are, in fact, revolutionary bases of the Johnson operation.

Kim Carsons sets himself the task of "organiz[ing] the Johnson Family into an all-out worldwide space program" (102). Only in space can the Johnsons transcend the oppressive control systems of the heterocapitalist world. According to Kim Earth has reached an evolutionary dead end, a state of "Arrested Evolution" (40). Only in space can they escape the oppressive influence of the Harts and Bickfords, who represent the heterocapitalist machinery, and be able to further the evolutionary process of humanity. As Burroughs wrote, "The Johnson family formulates a Manichean position where good and evil are in conflict and the outcome is at this point uncertain. It is *not* an eternal conflict, since one or the other must win a final victory" (*Adding Machine,* 74). Barry Miles summarized this "Manichean" conflict when he argued that "the theme of the book" is "the Johnson Family versus the shits" (*William Burroughs* 228). Burroughs, in typical fashion, described the nature of the "shits" in terms of a virus that causes the "shits" to believe themselves infallible: "Now your virus is an obligate parasite, and my contention is that what we call evil is quite literally a virus parasite occupying a certain brain area which we may term the RIGHT center. The mark of your basic shit is that he has to be *right*" (*Place of Dead Roads* 155). The "shits" believe themselves to be infallible, and they attempt to force this "rightness" on those they designate as "abject." As Burroughs made clear, one side must inevitably obliterate the other; the Johnsons, however, remain grossly outnumbered by the "shits." Burroughs described the vast gulf between the numbers of Johnsons and "shits" in his introduction to *Queer,* when he tells a story about searching for a pharmacy to take his "narcotics script": "Yes, you found a Johnson, but you waded through Shitville to find him. You always do. Just when you think the earth is exclusively populated by Shits, you meet a Johnson" (x).

To win this "Manichean" conflict between the Johnsons and the "shits" and escape from Earth into space, the Johnsons "seek a Total Solution to the Shit Problem: Slaughter the shits of the world like cows with the aftosa" (155).

Jamie Russell pointed out the disturbingly fascist overtones of Kim Carsons's proposed "Total Solution to the Shit Problem" using his "Shit Slaughter brigades": "In *The Place of Dead Roads,* allusions to fascism are taken even further; Kim Carsons' hatred of 'civilization'—that is, the religious, prohibitive, feminine 'law' of the frontier towns he inhabits—leads him to fantasize a program of 'Shit Slaughter,' a mass purgation of all who oppose his brand of queer self-reliance" (Russell 129). While these fascist ideas are disturbing, destroying the "shits" is essential to bringing about Marx and Engels's "total disappearance of class antagonisms." The victory of space over time, as de Certeau made clear, requires the creation of a space designated as "proper," from which a revolutionary group's "strategies" can be enacted. If their revolutionary schemes are to succeed, the Johnsons must first create a base of operations, de Certeau's "proper," from which they can operate on equal terms with the "shits."

Kim explains the importance of mimicry in his revolutionary plan when he says, "If you wish to conceal something it is necessary to create disinterest in the area where it is hidden"; thus Kim "planned towns, areas, communities, owned and operated by the Johnsons, that would appear to outsiders as boringly ordinary or disagreeable, that would leave no questions unanswered" (130). One problem, however, that the Johnsons have with passing for an ordinary town is that the Johnson Family, except for Salt Chunk Mary, is a purely male homosexual group. As in Port Roger, for a town to pass as normal it obviously needs a female population as well.

Like the Iguana Girl and Hirondelle de Mer in *Cities,* the character of Salt Chunk Mary poses something of a conundrum to the ultramasculine, antifeminine order of the Johnsons; she is, however, the most positive female character in Burroughs's entire body of work. But, as Barry Miles pointed out, her major scene in *Dead Roads* is "a complete re-run of her role in Jack Black's *You Can't Win*" (*William Burroughs* 226). Mary functions as a tough, masculinized version of women, yet it still seems that Burroughs drew her mostly as a homage to a favorite book from his childhood than as any kind of tribute to the potential of the female sex. Timothy Murphy claimed that "women occupy an ambivalent position in *The Place of Dead Roads,* as both allies . . . and enemies" (*Wising Up the Marks* 187). Other than the apparently nostalgic inclusion of Salt Chunk Mary, the place of women does not seem that "ambivalent" in the novel because, as it states, "Women must be regarded as the principal reservoir of the virus parasite. Women and religious sons of bitches. Above all, religious women" (97). The virus spoken of here is an alien virus from the planet Venus that Kim believes to be the source of all the control mechanisms that the Johnsons are battling. The aliens use the virus to breed the control apparatuses that Kim so adamantly opposes because the aliens support "any dogmatic religious system that tends to stupefy and degrade the worshippers," all forms of "dogmatic authority," the "inver[sion]" of "human values," "the arch-conservatives," and, according to Burroughs, they are solely responsible for the Industrial Revolution (97). Since women are the main virus carriers, they represent everything against which the Johnsons are struggling, and they cannot be allowed to infiltrate Johnsonville or the other Johnson communes.

The characters throughout the "Red Night" texts thus seek ways of creating their all-male homosexual utopias without the need of women to reproduce. Robin Lyndenberg summarized Burroughs's viewpoint on the male/female dichotomy as the source of virtually all social evils: "Burroughs attributes the polarization of reproductive energy to structures of binary opposition which set two incompatible sexes in perpetual conflict, channeling the flow of creative energy into a parasitic economy based on power and property" (156). Therefore the entire capitalistic system maintains itself based on this binary opposition of the sexes, and, as Jamie Russell pointed out, "the texts argue for the total separation of the masculine and feminine spheres, even going so far as to characterize American society as matriarchal" (92). To escape from this matriarchal society, Burroughs's characters do attempt to separate these "spheres" by creating utopian societies composed entirely of men while still maintaining the ability to reproduce.

Unlike Port Roger, Kim Carsons and the Johnsons seek the total exclusion of women—even as purely reproductive vessels—from their utopias. The Johnsons contend that women are unnecessary for reproduction; as Kim states, "We will give all our attention to experiments designed to produce asexual offspring, to cloning, use of artificial wombs, and transfer operations" (98). Indeed the Johnsons do manage to clone themselves successfully, as has already been seen. Although the Johnsons can eradicate the need for women in their society, the lack of women poses serious problems for Johnsonville's ability to seem like a normal town, and this eventually causes it to be unable to completely pass as an ordinary western town. When Colonel Sutton Smith, a "highly placed operative of British intelligence," comes to town to conduct archaeological research, he notices troubling aspects of the town (147). While Kim's idea of a community "that looks like any other town to the outsider" holds up from afar, the facade quickly breaks down under close scrutiny. Smith, as he relates in his diary, first recognizes Johnsonville as nothing other than "archetypical for middle American towns of this size"; however, he soon begins to notice strange aspects of the locals: "Am I imagining things or is there something just a bit too typical about Johnsonville? And why do the women all have big feet?" (148). Apparently, despite Kim's assertion that "we can hardly get away with stocking a whole town with female impersonators," the town is indeed populated exclusively by men, who play the roles of heterosexual men and women. Smith also notices that the inhabitants of Johnsonville play out the same tired scenes repeatedly, but, before he can act against the Johnsons, the sheriff determines his true identity as a British agent and coerces him into cooperating with the Johnsons. The Johnsons probably seem like normal middle Americans to any casual passersby, but astute observers such as Smith can notice the idiosyncrasies in the behavior of the townspeople.

Although the Johnsons seek to rid themselves of effeminacy, they also use it to their advantage in various strategies in the novel that involve passing as women or as straight men, and they even play with straight heteronormative stereotypes. As Russell explained, they use the "dominant stereotype of the 'fag,'" as a sort of "Trojan Horse tactic" when The Wild Fruits become involved in a gunfight (92). While staying at the "hacienda of the Fuentes family," Kim and the Wild Fruits "find trunks full of female clothes" (98). They dress up in drag and travel to the local village: "Kim calls himself the Green Nun, and Tom does Pious Señora, and Boy is the blushing Señorita" (99). The sheriff and the other inhabitants of the village, particularly the Jefe, "know something is going on up at the hacienda" and already have a strong hatred for Kim and the other Wild Fruits (99). Passing as women provides Kim and the other Wild Fruits with a momentary advantage, and they subsequently cast off their female garb and kill everyone in sight. Other Johnsons also use heteronormative stereotypes to carry out secret missions. Greg and Brad, "two American queens," play into the stereotype of the effeminate and style-conscious homosexual by "run[ning] an antique store and do[ing] decorating jobs" (223). However, Burroughs made clear that they are inherently masculine when he described them as "Johnson Agents, better trained than any secret service in the world, with the exception of the Japanese ninja" (223). Despite their various strategies to create propers or to transform stereotypes into subversive strategies, the Johnsons strategy ultimately fails. Burroughs must finally envision a strategy that applies to every person of abject status, a status that women have always hovered around since they have been forced to adhere to male-defined roles throughout history.

After viewing the examples of revolutionary practice in the first two "Red Night" novels, the reader must question whether or not Burroughs's new subversive strategies prove viable. Ultimately the revolutionary praxis of the first two "Red Night" novels does not prove as radical as Burroughs probably hoped it would. Jamie Russell stated that "the overriding problem with which Burroughs' masculine queer fantasy presents the reader is its unfaltering reliance on a definition of the masculine based upon heterosexual models. . . . Many of the desires voiced in Burroughs' texts replicate the exclusion, denial, or rejection of the feminine that some male American literature has repeatedly put forward, although the presentation of this in Burroughs is always queer" (135). Burroughs's attempts to subvert heterosexual hegemony always prove faulty because of the reification of the masculine paradigm that a true subversive would also seek to break down. Indeed in this passage Russell placed Burroughs in the long line of American novelists who simply could see no point in giving a voice to the feminine side of society or of their selves. However, more than just failing to effect a complete revolution from a queer-feminist perspective, *Cities of the Red Night* and *The Place of Dead Roads* also prove incapable of bringing about a satisfactory revolution on their own terms.

The endings of the first two novels of the trilogy mirror each other, as do their beginnings. Both novels begin with a supposedly historical account that has immediate importance to the plotlines of the novels: *Cities of the Red Night* begins with the retelling of the story of Captain Mission's eighteenth-century pirate commune, and *The Place of Dead Roads* starts with a nineteenth-century newspaper account of a gunfight involving Kim Carsons. Both novels also feature the lead characters blowing rents in the fabric of time itself, albeit at different points in the novels. Audrey, in the last words of *Cities of the Red Night,* states, "I have a blown a hole in time with a firecracker. Let others step through. Into what bigger and bigger firecrackers? Better weapons lead to better and better weapons until the earth is a grenade with the fuse burning" (332). Audrey manages to free himself and any who can "get through the gate in time" from the constraints of time, thereby providing the potential for moving into space; however, movement through space, as Burroughs made clear throughout the trilogy, requires freeing one's self from the physical confines of the body.

Later in the novel, Burroughs wrote, "Happiness is a by-product of function. Those who seek happiness for itself seek victory without war. This is the flaw in all utopias" (237). Burroughs's characters, of course, do not shy away from all-out war; they are not pacifist utopians, and they do not seek to avoid war at all costs like Sir Thomas More's Utopians, thus rendering them exempt from this common utopian flaw. To support his claims, Burroughs quoted Nietzsche: "Men need play and danger" (217).

Indeed, Kim, Audrey, the Johnsons, and all of Burroughs's revolutionary characters embody the antiherd mentality and the attempt to escape beyond the binary of good and evil that Nietzsche discusses in *Beyond Good and Evil* (1886): "Throughout Europe the herding animal alone attains to honours, when 'equality of right' can too readily be transformed into equality of wrong; I mean to say into general war against everything rare, strange, and privileged, against the higher man, the higher soul, the higher duty, the higher responsibility, the creative plenipotence and lordliness—at present it belongs to the conception of 'greatness' to be noble, to wish to be apart, to be capable of being different, to stand alone" (84). The Johnsons and the pirates of Port Roger no doubt attain the Nietzschean status of "greatness" because they have rejected the herd mentality of subjectification and chose abjectivity instead. The "Red Night" characters are obviously not concerned with the ideal of "happiness," nor do they fear the battlefield or seek "victory without war." Their only failure as revolutionaries stems from a much more metaphysical dilemma.

In the final analysis, Burroughs's utopian vision in *Cities of the Red Night* and *The Place of Dead Roads* does not prevail because the hegemonic machinery is never completely destroyed. Barbara Rose, in her article on conspiracy and paranoia in *Cities of the Red Night,* concluded that "Burroughs's last paranoid narratives . . . arrive at the greatest conspiratorial fear: that there is no center, no source to the conspiracy, and thus no possibility of resolution or closure" (93). For example the ending of *The Place of Dead Roads,* which is a reworking of the novel's opening in which Kim Carsons takes part in a shootout with Mike Chase, does not provide the hopes of escape that the beginning sequence offers. After Kim has gunned down Mike Chase, he "shoots a hole in the moon, a black hole with fuzz around it like powder burns," similar to Audrey's hole in reality at the end of *Cities of the Red Night* (*Place of Dead Roads* 8). After taking another shot, "all the spurious old father figures rush on stage" with screams of "YOU'RE DESTROYING THE UNIVERSE" to which Kim responds,

> "What universe?"
>
> Kim shoots a hole in the sky. Blackness pours out and darkens the earth. In the last rays of a painted sun, a Johnson holds up a barbed-wire fence for others to slip through. The fence has snagged the skyline . . . a great black rent. Screaming crowds point to the torn sky.
>
> "OFF THE TRACK! OFF THE TRACK!"
>
> "FIX IT!" the director bellows . . .
>
> "What with, a Band-Aid and chewing gum? Rip in the Master Film . . . Fix it Yourself, Boss MAN."
>
> "ABANDON SHIP, GOD DAMN IT. . . . EVERY MAN FOR HIMSELF!" (9)

The novel's opening hearkens back to one of Burroughs's controlling metaphors in his earlier fiction, particularly in the cut-ups: the idea of the master reality film. Burroughs's *Paris Review* interview also includes the author explaining his conceptualization of reality as a biological film when asked about the significance of the "Grey Room":

> I see it very much like the photographic darkroom where the reality photographs are actually produced. Implicit in *Nova Express* is a theory that what we call reality is actually a movie. It's a film, what I call a biologic film. What has happened is that the underground and also the nova police have made a breakthrough past the guards and gotten into the darkroom where the films are processed, where they're in a position to expose negatives and prevent events from occurring. (*Beat Writers at Work* 16)

Indeed when Kim shoots a hole in the sky and knocks the film off its track, the reader familiar with the Cut-Up trilogy almost expects to hear the constant refrain from the Nova trilogy, which Burroughs constantly presented in slightly different permutations: "Photo falling—word falling—Break Through in Grey Room—Use Partisans of all nations—Towers, open fire—" (*Nova Express* 59). Thus at the beginning of the novel Kim seems to have the power to break through the reality film, to rewrite history, to stop the increasing industrialization and capitalization at the end of the nineteenth century, and to escape from the prison of time like Audrey Carsons; however, the beginning and the ending of the novel tell different stories.

The Place of Dead Roads opens with two 1899 newspaper clippings about a shootout between author Kim Carson and Mike Chase and an 1894 newspaper article about Carsons's gang, describing how Kim wins the shootout by making Mike draw his gun too fast: "Suddenly Kim flicks his hand up without drawing as he points at Mike with his index finger. 'BANG! YOU'RE DEAD.' He throws the last word like a stone. He knows that Mike will *see* a gun in the empty hand and this will crowd his draw" (7). Indeed Kim's finger causes Mike to draw "much too fast," and Mike's bullet "whistles past his left shoulder" (7). Thus Kim has ample time to draw and aim properly, and "Kim's bullet hits Mike just above the heart with a liquid SPLAT as the mercury explodes inside, blowing the aorta to shreds" (7–8). Kim proceeds to blow holes in the sky and send the reality film screeching off its tracks, breaking the destiny of future human events preordained by the control machine.

The novel's end features the same shootout between Kim and Mike and the same ruse on Kim's part, yet events work out differently in this second version. The second shootout takes up much less space in the text but begins similarly: "Kim's hand flicks down to his holster and up, hand empty, pointing his index finger at Mike. 'BANG! YOU'RE DEAD' Mike clutches his chest and crumples forward in a child's game" (306). In this version Kim never actually shoots Mike; he pretends to shoot, just as Mike pretends to be shot. However, the disturbing part comes in the next lines, the last ones of the novel: "'WHAT THE FU—' Someone slaps Kim very hard on the back, knocking the word out. Kim *hates* being slapped on the back. He turns in angry protest . . . blood in his mouth . . . can't turn . . . the sky darkens and goes out" (*Place of Dead Roads* 306). Without having read *The Western Lands* as well, the first-time reader probably is unsure of what exactly has transpired at the end of *The Place of Dead Roads*. Only the blood in Kim's mouth and the fact that he "can't turn" point to the fact that he has been shot from behind by an unknown assailant.

Kim's subterfuge in the novel's opening, which promises the revolutionary potential that the rest of the novel expounds on, does not retain its effectiveness at the novel's closing. Instead Mike falls down and plays dead, a move that leaves Kim unable to shoot, while an unseen sniper shoots Kim from behind. The novel's end portrays the "evil old men" winning by having learned to use Kim's own "strategies" against him and by buying out one of his compatriots, Joe the Dead, who Burroughs revealed in *The Western Lands* to be Kim's assassin. Early in *The Western Lands*, Burroughs replayed the ending of *The Place of Dead Roads*, but he focuses on the sniper this time instead: "Joe the Dead lowered the rifle. . . . Behind him, Kim Carsons and Mike Chase lay dead in the dust of the Boulder Cemetery. The date was September 17, 1899" (26). The death of Kim Carsons at the close *The Place of Dead Roads* reveals the only true path of escape from control: death. Only by breaking the bonds of the body can the subject be freed from all constraints that society places on him or her. However, even the afterlife, as the final volume of the trilogy reveals, contains control mechanisms that attempt to govern who is allowed to enter the Western Lands.

Control Even in Death: Reaching for Utopia in *The Western Lands*

Timothy Murphy called *The Western Lands* "the tale that Burroughs had tried to tell, in various forms, for his entire career" (*Wising Up the Marks* 200). *The Western Lands* reveals that if one is to escape from control, then one must first escape from the body on which biopower exercises its control via the circuit of time. Only escape from fear and the body guarantees a person's entrance into the Western Lands and an immortality free from control. The Western Lands, however, are also subject to the forces of control because they have been monopolized by the vampiric mummies—the pharaohs of Ancient Egypt and the capitalists of the modern world—thus Kim Carsons, Neferti, Hassan i Sabbah, William Seward Hall, and, consequently, William S. Burroughs must seek to expose the ways of gaining access to the Western Lands and of breaking the monopoly on immortality:

> The road to the Western Lands is the most dangerous of all roads and, in consequence, the most rewarding. To know the road exists violates the

> human covenant: you are not allowed to confront fear, pain and death, or to find out that sacred human covenant was signed under pressure of fear, pain and death. They can keep their covenant in case of being short with a million years of bullshit. To enter the Western Lands means leaving the covenant behind in the human outhouse with the Monkey Ward catalogues. (*Western Lands* 180)

The characters in *The Western Lands* seek to—and Burroughs himself sought to—illuminate the way to the Western Lands for the general populace and to smash the "exclusive country club" of immortality (196). To do this they must train people to exist without "fear, pain and death" and also without the body. Only then is space travel possible, and only then can people truly become free from control. Although the revolutionary strategy of *Cities of the Red Night* and *The Place of Dead Roads* does not entirely succeed, Burroughs apparently believed that *The Western Lands* achieved the revolutionary strategy he had been developing since he began writing novels, because the novel ends with the statement: "The old writer couldn't write anymore because he had reached the end of words, the end of what can be done with words" (258).

In *The Western Lands,* the reader glimpses one last group of revolutionaries creating their own "proper" in order to counteract the repressive control forces of the rich and elite. Again the characters in *The Western Lands* employ strategies against the pharaoh, who holds a monopoly on immortality in the afterlife. The pharaoh can detect "a dagger in your mind"; thus Neferti uses a sort of telepathic camouflage in order to cloak his revolutionary agenda from the pharaoh: "Neferti knows the arts of telepathic blocking and misdirection. You can't make your mind a blank, for that would be detected at once. You must present a cover mind which the Pharaoh can tune into, and which is completely harmless: 'For me the Pharaoh is God.' You can't lay it on too thick" (104). Typical of his comedy, Burroughs mocked the desire of rulers to be the objects of flattery; however, simultaneously, he again revealed the importance of hiding one's motives from the higher authorities. Even when the body has been left behind, the abject revolutionary must learn how to use his or her mind to break through the final channels of control. Indeed the mind becomes the final proper from which individuals, freed from control's dividualization, create bases of operation within their minds.

The pharaohs and their immortal forms, mummies—which Burroughs always stressed possess a vampiric nature—represent the source of control in the novel and, thus, are cast in the role of the primary enemies against whom Neferti and the others on the path to the Western Lands must struggle. Engaging in the subversive act called "Secret Painting," Neferti's tribe must, like Kim

Carsons, "create disinterest in the area where it is hidden"—that is, they must create a "proper" that passes as nondescript to any chance outsiders: "their haunts are not secret in the sense of being hidden. To the outsider they would appear as a perfectly ordinary house or inn. Should an unwanted stranger happen in, he will see nothing noteworthy, but rather an emptiness, a lack of anything that can engage his interest or pleasure" (*Western Lands* 105). The revolutionaries—like the Port Roger pirates and the Johnsons—conceal their base of operations from outside interference through the strategy of passing as normal, of creating disinterest in the proper (the home base of revolutionary activity); that is, by hiding in plain sight. In response to the increased vampiric visitations of the mummies, the revolution begins to spread quickly. Providing another bleakly comical image of absolute control, Burroughs described these visitations of the vampires on the *fellaheen*—the lower-class citizens subjected to the absolute rule of the pharaoh—in scenes reminiscent of the succubi and incubi of Judeo-Christian mythology: "A certain species of vampire which can take male or female form sneaks into the rooms of youths. The pleasures they offer are irresistible, and the victim is hopelessly captivated by these nightly visits which no lock or charm can forestall. The victim loses all interest in human contact. He lives only for the visits of the vampire, which leave him always weaker and more wasted. In the end he is little more than a living mummy" (106). Like the mugwumps, these vampires create addicts and are revealed to be "the ghosts of mummies who immortalize themselves this way and convert the energy required to maintain the Western Lands" and succeed in further inciting the citizens to revolution. Mementot, one of the leaders of the revolution, provides the battle cry of the partisans: "I am going to destroy every fucking mummy I get my hands on. The Western Lands of the rich are watered by *fellaheen* blood, built of *fellaheen* flesh and bones, lighted by *fellaheen* spirit" (106). Thus, the age-old battle between the classes continues into the afterlife, where the immortal pharaohs still exert control over both the land of the dead and the land of the living.

Eventually the pharaohs' and priests' absolute control of the Western Lands begins to loosen when the afterlife "open[s] to the middle class of merchants and artisans, speculators and adventurers, pimps, grave robbers and courtesans" (160). Cheaper mummies are introduced, "cut-rate embalmers" who "offer pay-as-you-go plans," and "Embalming Conclaves" that produce mummies through an assembly line method leads to complete commodification of immortality in *The Western Lands* (160–61). The pharaoh, of course, still wields control over this commodifying of eternal life, but he is willing to let it proceed in order to continue to exercise his control over the lower and middle classes. The priests, on the other hand, are initially alarmed at the prospect "of a hideous soul glut"; however, the pharaoh, recognizing the need for the middle class as a potential army because of threats of "invasion from without and rebellion from within," decides "to throw the biggest sop he's got to the middle classes, to ensure their loyalty" (161). Thus he gives the middle classes the gift of immortality, but he retains the ability to oust them from eternal life at a later date if necessary: "If things get rough, we can always liquidate the excess mummies" (161). The lower class—the *fellaheen*—also manages to find passage into the Western Lands by performing "embalmings in their fish-drying sheds and smokehouses" (161). Through thriftiness the nonelite classes manage to disrupt the mummy monopoly that had previously been maintained by the pharaohs and their simpering priests—they appropriate the methods of their oppressors as strategies for attacking the control system.

The pharaohs cannot grant access to all who would seek entrance to the Western Lands because, as Burroughs reiterated, "the Western Lands are fashioned from mud, from fellaheen death, from the energy released at the time of Death" (196). The *fellaheen* must continue to die in order for the "exclusive country club" that is the Western Lands to be maintained (196). On his journey through the Land of the Dead and toward the Western Lands, Kim Carsons learns how this system of control can be bypassed—through the eradication of the reliance on the "parasitic female Other Half that needs a physical body to exist" (74). Kim comes to understand that this is the reason why the pharaohs rely on the preservation of the physical form and the consequent vampirism that this entails. Kim and the other male homosexual heroes of the novel learn to subvert this system by reaching the Western Lands through "the contact of two males"; thus "the myth of duality is exploded and the initiates can realize their natural state. The Western Lands is the natural, uncorrupted state of all male humans. We have been seduced from our biologic and spiritual destiny by the Sex Enemy" (74–75). The Western Lands, then, represent yet another male homosexual utopia, and Burroughs's misogyny persists even into his last great novel.

In Burroughs's oeuvre it becomes necessary for characters to learn methods of escaping from the confines of their physical forms, to learn ways of breaking the body and subverting the binary system of biological sexual representation that it entails. By making themselves "less solid," the partisan revolutionaries can combat the agents of the vampiric mummy control and create their own Western Lands, in which elitism has been completely banished: "Look at their Western Lands. What do they look like? The houses and gardens of a rich man. Is this all the gods can offer. Well I say it is time for new Gods who do not offer such paltry bribes. . . . We can make our own Western Lands" (164). The question, then, arises of how to make this new Western Lands solid and not merely a "Land of Dreams," but solidity is the last thing that the revolutionaries want because that was "the error of the mummies"—"they made spirit solid" (165). Thus the reader glimpses Kim Carsons and his compatriots moving into space as beings of light to engage their enemies. The novel then proceeds into a parody of "The Charge of the Light Brigade"; however, unlike Tennyson's poem, here the soldiers are not simply fast, but are actually made of light. Being made solely of light allows the partisans to maintain "the element of surprise" because "the virus enemy cannot comprehend elasticity" (175). They, thus, are capable of operating outside the "seemingly foolproof broadcasts" of the enemy, rendering them virtually invulnerable to the agents of control (175).

The partisans, through the loss of their bodies, manage to escape from what Foucault calls "a policy of coercions that act upon the body, a calculated manipulation of its elements, its gestures, its behavior" (138). For Foucault the body was one of the primary sites on which control acted "not only so that they may do what one wishes, but so that they may operate as one wishes, with the techniques, the speed and the efficiency that one determines" (138). Power, thus, conditions the body to not only be "docile," in Foucault's words, but to perform its designated tasks within society, whether it be factory work, soldiering, or intellectual labor (138). By eradicating this site of repression, the revolutionaries of *The Western Lands* can wage all-out war on the agents of control without any fear of being sucked back into the matrices of power. They are able to succeed where Burroughs's previous revolutionaries had failed. No doubt the success of the revolution in *The Western Lands* led Burroughs to feel he had finally accomplished the task that he had set for himself in the late 1950s when he began writing *Naked Lunch:* he had finally found a way for his characters to exist completely beyond the reach of power, prompting the concluding passage of the novel in which "the old writer couldn't write anymore because he had reached the end of words, the end of what can be done with words" (258).

CHAPTER 7

Love

The Final Revolutionary Force

Burroughs never produced another work that lived up to the level of the Red Night trilogy, and many considered *The Western Lands* to be his swan song. However, he continued to produce a variety of decidedly minor but fascinating texts up through the time of his death: these range from prose to paintings to musical collaborations, and other forms. While he devoted the bulk of his late-life artistic endeavors to painting, he still produced some prose works worth considering here because they espouse the final version of his revolutionary theory. After all the years of Burroughs being the hard-edged revolutionary figure, these later texts begin to present the reader with a softer side of Burroughs, with a new viewpoint that he espouses in his two animal-centered novels, *The Cat Inside* and *Ghost of Chance*. His final published works before his death were *My Education* and *Last Words,* a collection of his final journals. All these works, whether fictional or not, begin to explore the power of love versus apathy or cruelty or both. Burroughs's later works boil the Johnson code down to the essential golden rule of "Love thy neighbor as thyself"; however for Burroughs this ethical formulation serves as the basis for resisting control and re-creating ourselves anew.

For many *The Western Lands* ended the Burroughs's mythology that stretched back to *Junky*. However, in 1986 Burroughs published a slim volume about his family of cats called *The Cat Inside,* which begins to direct his revolutionary agenda in a new direction. The characters in *The Western Lands* actively seek death as the final space of freedom. *The Cat Inside,* on the other hand, opens with a birth that signals a new direction for Burroughs albeit one that remains in line with the Johnson code. Whereas the Johnsons participated in a cooperative yet individualistic ethics with revolution as its driving force, *The Cat Inside* begins to demonstrate how love may actually be the revolutionary force that Burroughs had been seeking all along.

The Cat Inside concerns revolution on a much smaller scale: the elimination of quotidian suffering and pain experienced by beings other than humans that people ignore daily. The novella (or journal—it is difficult to determine its genre) provided a mournful, tender, regretful side of Burroughs that readers had never seen before. Burroughs became increasingly appalled at the human animal and its cruelty. In his previous writings, Burroughs had argued that the human constituted an evolutionary dead end that demanded escape from the body. However, *The Cat Inside* shows Burroughs learning to embrace a less transcendent form of evolution, one in which humankind relinquishes its role at the top of the food chain, as the apex predator who can torment and destroy whole species at its will. Indeed humankind resides at the top of the food chain only because of its ability to wield tools and weapons. But this actually provides a new mutation (or evolution) of Burroughs's own theories about the evolutionary blockage that is the human condition. Throughout the book Burroughs grieved continually because of the horrors that are cruelty and death, and perhaps it requires a transcendence beyond the body to achieve a state in which humankind becomes capable of casting off such horrid attributes of itself. Burroughs even began to consider other forms of life beyond the kingdom Animalia, such as bacteria, which even led him to question whether viruses constitute a form of life since they are nothing more than DNA wrapped in a protein shell that is capable of infecting a host organism. Since they are labeled as inactive agents, then are they alive? Is DNA the basic requirement for life, or is it something more? Burroughs's work here leaves the reader wondering about the nature of life itself and which lives deserve to be spared the cruelty that humankind has always been so willing to dish out against supposedly "lower life forms," a phrase that has been seriously challenged not just by animal rights groups but within philosophy and theory as well with fields such as posthuman theory and animal studies.

Another novella and Burroughs's final major work of fiction, *Ghost of Chance* features the reappearance of Captain Mission and Mr. Martin as Mission attempts to set up an outpost in Madagascar and protect the lemur population. Similarly many of Burroughs's major themes also return: time, viruses, language, and others. However, Burroughs's tone has shifted slightly to incorporate a new kind of compassion and desire for conservation—the book even includes a call for help at the end, the first time that Burroughs's works openly states a position on a sociocultural issue. Captain Mission establishes a settlement in Madagascar where the lemurs are regarded as sacred animals—the indigenous word for lemur meant ghost—and it was taboo to kill them. Therefore Captain Mission also forbids his men to harm the lemurs. His quest is to discover a rumored larger species of lemur. During his ramblings he comes across Bradly Martin and the corpse of a lemur, which he had shot for stealing his mango. Mission exiles him from Libertatia for his crime, but he constantly feels Martin's destructive presence lurking on the island.

Mission begins to spend an increasing amount of time in the forest with the lemurs and even begins to sleep cuddled up with them (in a nonsexual fashion). This was actually a fantasy of Burroughs's—to have a giant lemur to cuddle with in bed. The narrator explains that "the Lemur people are older than Homo Sap . . . their way of thinking and feeling is basically different from ours, not oriented toward time and sequence and causality. They find these concepts repugnant and difficult to understand" (15). The lemur, therefore, provides another example of being freed from time: "Time is a human affliction; not a human invention but a prison. . . . Man was born in time. He lives and dies in time. Wherever he goes, he takes time with him and imposes time" (16–17). Time, of course, implies control, and since the Lemur People exist without time, then, they must either submit to time or be destroyed.

Because Mission champions freedom from time and control, he must also be subdued. After receiving a report of an impending sea attack on his settlement, he takes to the sea but then discovers this was only a ruse. He returns to find his settlement burning, and his favorite lemur, Ghost, dies in his arms. Burroughs then returns to the cinematic metaphor for the most dramatic scene in the story:

> The Entrance . . . an old film . . . dim, grainy explosive charge . . . plaintive paw up to his face. . . . He knows I am a hundred and sixty million years away . . . torn roots like broken hands . . . a sad, weak cry.
>
> This grief can kill, but Captain Mission is a soldier. He will not surrender to the enemy. With an agonizing wrench his grief forms an imprecation. He transmutes his grief into an incandescent blaze of hate and calls down a curse on the Boards and the Martins of the world, on all their servants, dupes, and followers:
>
> "I will loose on them the blood of Christ!" (21–22)

Christ may seem like a strange choice for a Burroughs character to invoke in a curse. Why not Ah Pook or some other occult deity; however, *Ghost* elaborates on Mission's curse by providing some hypothetical first-person stories from Jesus himself.

In the first story, a man comes to Jesus with a sick monkey and asks Jesus to heal it, but Jesus explains that he cannot heal the monkey because animals do not have souls. The man responds, "*They have grace and beauty and innocence. What are the people you heal but animals?*" Jesus explains that he cannot "*heal him because he knows not Me and he knows not of Him who sent Me.*" Consequently the man denounces Christ: "*Then I care nothing for You, nor for Him who sent You. For He sent You to make Men less than they are not more. He sent you to blind our eyes and stop our ears*" (24). The man's condemnation of Christ hearkens back to Nietzsche, who despised any form of morality that enslaved men's minds—Christ, then, comes to represent another form of control, another cog in the control machinery. The book ends with a call to action to help protect lemurs from those who deem them unworthy of consideration. Burroughs considers them to be on a level with human beings. The only difference is that humankind has oral and written traditions. Burroughs quotes his old favorite Korzybski, who stated that "man is a time-binding animal." The lemur, thus, provides Burroughs's final image of freedom from control—the lemur cares nothing about time and hence cares nothing about control. It is free to live as it pleases with no one forcing morality on it. The only problem resides in humankind's ability to wantonly destroy that which is deemed to have no use or exchange value.

The last major work published during his lifetime, *My Education: A Book of Dreams* follows in the unique tradition of dream diaries, which Kerouac also participated in with his own *Book of Dreams*. Burroughs acknowledged at the beginning of the book that other people's dreams are boring to listen to, and he is not wrong, but he proceeds to provide a tour of his dream world nonetheless. Aside from his letters, his South American journals, his late journals (to be discussed below), and *The Cat Inside, My Education* provides an interesting insight into Burroughs's internal world. Burroughs always maintained that he was a lucid, active dreamer capable of recognizing when he was in a dream and bending it to his will. Furthermore he always maintained that much of his writing derived from dreams and the dream journal that he kept. The surrealists always placed particular importance on dreams and tried to recreate them in many of their works, and Burroughs provides a similar experience, using his dreams to help craft the fantastic and horrific backdrops against which his stories take place as well as the characters that populate these spaces.

In *Paradise Outlaws,* John Tyell explained that, after many meetings with Burroughs, he discovered that only one thing interested Burroughs: his interior consciousness, thus leading to his abuse of drugs, his dabbling in scientology and the occult, his use of the orgone box, and his attempts to break free from language's control via cut-ups and other methods. As has been seen before, Burroughs always argued that humanity must escape time and embrace space, but it is interior space not exterior space to which Burroughs refers. As with the lucid dreamer, a freedom from the body allows the user to embrace his interior space and bend it to his will, to explore realms, emotions, and experiences beyond comprehension. Humans' past combines with their present and all the possibilities beyond the two to create a new kind of consciousness, a new image of thought, to refer back to Deleuze, in which being finally gets completely replaced by constant active becoming, by a rhizomatic existence escaping down endless lines of flight. However, lines of flight prove unnecessary because disembodiment frees the subject from time and control. The reality proscribed by control vanishes in the rearview as the subject relinquishes its place in linearity, language, and control. He creates his own reality as free as he wants it to be.

While *My Education* can be read as a kind of autobiography of the mind, *Last Words* proves more problematic because of its posthumous publication. Aside from the Latin American journals that were recently published, the public has never seen Burroughs's journals in the way that they have Kerouac's or Ginsberg's. The critical value of *Last Words* further upholds Burroughs's theories about love as a revolutionary force. As with *The Cat Inside,* a softer side of Burroughs is visible in these journals. The journals, which start on November 14, 1996, open like a continuation of *The Cat Inside* with a report of his cat that had been discovered dead: "In the empty spaces where the cat was, that hurt *physically.* Cat is part of me" (1).[1] Starting from this sentimental moment in which Burroughs again demonstrates his late-life capacity for genuine love, the book continues to feature records of the day's activities, short routines, and memories. Despite his new emotional capacity, Burroughs still remained strong and biting in his critique of issues such as the War on Drugs, which he found to be ludicrous and deadly: "Mark it to its place: it's *EVIL* and it means no good for anything Homo (experiment) Sap can or will create of value. It is here to exterminate" (29–30). Even in his last year of life, Burroughs viewed *Homo sapiens* as a failed evolutionary experiment, one that was not only trapped by its very biological nature but by control as well—the fight against drugs has only intensified since the Harrison Act was passed much earlier in his life. Now heavily armed U.S. police and immigration officers fight epic battles with brutal international drug cartels that wield weapons of equal power. His contempt for blatant hypocrisy became even more apparent when he owned being a cultural icon: "I am an unabashed cultural Icon. I stand for the truth. I hate liars. My familiar is the White Cat, formed of searing white moonlight under which all hidden plots, all lies and deceits, are brought to the light of The Hunting Cat. He can't be bought. Stack it to the ceiling. He can't be scared. He is light right through. . . . What I mean by truth: I mean what is there when all the bullshit is gone. Not one lie left. All gone away" (38). These lines could easily summarize Burroughs's entire career from shining light on the lives of junkies and homosexual men to critiquing the nature of power to explicating the possibility of evolution beyond the human form. Familiars, of course, are associated with witchcraft and other occult practitioners. They were assistants of sorts, and the cat was one of the most common animals that superstition believed to be in the service of witches or even Satan himself. Black cats, in particular, were feared, and, in Goethe's *Faust,* Mephistopheles first appears to Faust in the form of a black cat.

Burroughs believed that the white cat might be a premonition of his own impending death, but he also claimed that it is "light right through," meaning that it remains free from the lies and hypocrisy that encrust the society of control. While he still continued his critique of the control society and its facade of goodwill, he also began to delve into the topic of love and its possibility for change or revolution. Burroughs discussed his loss of interest in sex: "Getting older I find the whole explicit subject of sex appalls me." Instead of sexual encounters, which Burroughs pursued in his youth, he now valued love and love of animals in particular. For him cats and lemurs provided his new metaphor for freedom from control—they are not mired in hypocritical morality, and they care nothing about society's opinion or its attempts to control them. Anyone who has ever tried to train a cat will quickly realize that their general response is "Fuck you! I will do what I goddamn well please!" Burroughs valued the cat for its grace and beauty but also for its independence—its refusal to become a slobbering sycophant like a dog. While the cat remains more apathetic, it still represents Burroughs's idea in the book of total dissent—the "total exposure of the dual human structure, which will entail *basic biological changes* of the human species" (63). Burroughs, thus, maintained his attitude of absolute resistance, but also his softening, weaker side. As he went to various doctors and grew older and weaker, he grappled not just with his own physical decline but with the death of his old friend Allen Ginsberg and two of his cats—the deaths of the cats were as horrible for Burroughs as any human's death. The journals end appropriately with a discussion of these two aspects of this late Burroughs. His July 18, 1997, entry opens with a statement of total dissent: "State of Hate of the Union. So many [divisions] of America are sunked in the vilest spiritual ignorance, stupidity and basic [ill intentions] toward anything, any potential Homo Sap may harbor. . . . The powder trail is there. All it needs is one spark" (241). Burroughs's use of the term "Homo Sap" always reminds the reader that the bulk of humankind are saps, marks that are manipulated by control without ever noticing the strings from which they dance (or hang, depending on control's assessment of their behavior). Burroughs spent his life as a writer and an artist trying to expose the strings of the control puppeteer, to drag humankind—screaming if necessary—out of the cave and into the light.

He has shown the way, but the people must be the ones to light the spark, to send the reality film spinning off track, to cut up the bullshit spectacle on all sides of the reader and reveal the computerized machinery of control that lies beneath. However, Burroughs's final words are not ones of violence; they are words of sadness and love, and he has reminded the reader that love cannot be forgotten along the way to revolution:

> "When you see the someone who looks like the saddest man in the world, that's him [Burroughs]."
> How can a mean who *sees* and *feels* be other than sad.
> To see Ginger [his cat] always older and weaker.
> The price of immortality, of course.
> Well, you should have thought of these things.
> I did. Thinking is not enough.
> Nothing is. There is no final enough of wisdom, experience—any fucking thing. No Holy Grail, No Final Satori, no final solution. Just conflict.
> Only thing that can resolve conflict is love, like I felt for Fletch and Ruski, Spooner and Calico [other cats]. Pure love.
> What I feel for my cats present and past.
> Love? What is it?
> Most natural painkiller that there is.
> LOVE. (252–53)

After all the years of cynical satire, visceral depictions of violence, and condemnations of society, the final word from Burroughs—at least the final word that his editors give the reader—is, ironically, *love*. Throughout his career Burroughs refined his definitions of control and the methods by which it might be resisted. He also theorized different possible forms of utopia, but ultimately the only thing that can make a society utopic is love, the love between fellow creatures. Only by means of this love can bonds be formed that can stand up to control and create society anew.

Epilogue

"Minutes to go, the heat are closing in"

One of the reasons that Burroughs has remained such a crucial figure to understanding contemporary literature, despite his death in 1997, is that each generation of authors, artists, and musicians rediscover Burroughs and appropriate his influence in new ways. From the hippies of the 1960s who grew out of the Beat Generation to punk musicians of the 1970s, the industrial pioneers and the cyberpunks of the 1980s, and even the grunge bands of the 1990s, artists have continued to be attracted to both the mystique of the Burroughs legend and the power of his works. Burroughs's persona, philosophy, and writings undoubtedly provide the major impetus for this admiration and emulation, but there is also the shock factor as well. The 1950s witnessed the publication of numerous works that began to alter the face of American fiction and that proved shocking at the time: J. D. Salinger's *The Catcher in the Rye,* Vladimir Nabokov's *Lolita* (1955), William Gaddis's *The Recognitions* (1955), Jack Kerouac's *On the Road,* and John Barth's *The Floating Opera* (1956) and *The End of the Road* (1958). These works all hearken back to high modernism, but they also exhibit the first inklings of the aesthetic shift that came to be known as postmodernism while also delving into subject matter that was taboo to the suburbanite facade of 1950s America. Aside from *Lolita,* which still raises some eyebrows, these works seem relatively tame today; however, Burroughs's work remains perennially shocking in a manner akin to that of the Marquis de Sade. Despite being written in the late eighteenth and early nineteenth centuries, de Sade's works remain as disturbing and pornographic today as they were upon their initial publication. De Sade, like Burroughs, also melded a carnivalesque, pornographic atmosphere together with a philosophical project that challenged the ideas of his time. The novels listed above also began to expand the limits of fictional form, but Burroughs forever shattered all previous modes of literature with his visceral, irreverent, and deconstructive style. Anyone interested in the history or theory of the novel must still grapple with the violent manner in which Burroughs assaulted not just the novel form but language itself. This genius instigated a seismic upheaval of the literary landscape that still resonates today throughout the various arts and philosophy. No matter how much technology has advanced or culture has changed, Burroughs's sense of the urgent need to combat a real and potent evil still bristles with electricity, inspiring each new generation of artists and thinkers in a variety of ways. We have only minutes to go, the heat are closing in, and Burroughs has the escape plan that we need because it is "time to look beyond this rundown radioactive cop-rotten planet" (*The Job*, 137).

NOTES

Chapter 1: Understanding William S. Burroughs

1. See Lyndenberg, *Word Cultures,* Murphy, *Wising up the Marks,* Weidner, *The Green Ghost,* and Fazzino, *World Beats,* respectively.

2. "Please Master" appears in *The Fall of America: Poems of These States, 1965–1971* (1973), which is number 30 in City Lights' Pocket Poets Series.

3. Like critic-theorist bell hooks, ruth weiss spelled her name with all lowercase letters.

Chapter 2: Desire and the Ugly Spirit

1. See his essay in Schneiderman and Walsh, *Retaking the Universe.*

2. *Yage* is often spelled with an accent mark (*yagé*), but Burroughs omits the accent mark in the title and throughout *The Yage Letters,* and that spelling has been used throughout.

3. Bogotá also has an accent mark that Burroughs leaves out, as does Policía Nacional.

4. Italics appear in the original text.

Chapter 3: The End of Their Forks

1. Burroughs frequently includes racial slurs to depict casual racism, particularly in individuals with positions of power such as "backwoods" sheriffs.

2. *Jouissance* literally means climaxing.

Chapter 4: Rub Out the Word

1. The double periods appear in the original.

2. Ellipsis appears in the text.

3. Italics and final dash appear in the original text.

4. Thanks to Timothy Murphy's book *Wising Up the Marks* for pointing to this Skerl quote.

5. The lowercase "i"s below appear in the original text.

6. Final dash appears in original text.

7. Single quotation marks appear in the original text.

8. The dash appears in the original text.

Chapter 7: Love

1. Italics appear in the original text.

SELECTED BIBLIOGRAPHY

Books by William S. Burroughs

The Adding Machine: Selected Essays. New York: Arcade, 1985.

Ah Pook Is Here and Other Texts. London: John Calder, 1979.

APO-33: A Metabolic Regulator. San Francisco: Beach Books, 1966.

Blade Runner: A Movie. Berkeley: Blue Wind, 1979.

The Burroughs File. San Francisco: City Lights Books, 1984.

Burroughs Live: The Collected Interviews of William S. Burroughs, 1960–1997. Ed. Sylvère Lotringer. Los Angeles: Semiotext(e), 2001.

The Cat Inside. New York: Viking, 1986.

Cities of the Red Night. New York: Henry Holt, 1981.

Concrete and Buckshot. Ed. Susan Martin. Santa Monica: Smart Art, 1996.

Conversations with William S. Burroughs. Ed. Allen Hibbard. Jackson: University Press of Mississippi, 1999.

Dead Fingers Talk. London: W. H. Allen, 1963.

The Electronic Revolution. Bonn: Expanded Media Edition, 1970.

Everything Lost: The Latin American Notebooks of William S. Burroughs. Ed. Geoffrey D. Smith, John M. Bennett, and Oliver Harris. Columbus: Ohio State University Press, 1992.

Exterminator! New York: Penguin, 1973.

The Four Horsemen of the Apocalypse. Bonn: Expanded Media Edition, 1979.

Ghost of Chance. New York: High Risk Books, 1991.

Interzone. Ed. James Grauerholz. New York: Penguin, 1989.

Junky: The Definitive Text of Junk. 1953. Ed. Oliver Harris. New York: Penguin, 2003.

The Last Words of Dutch Schultz. New York: Arcade, 1969.

Last Words: The Final Journals of William S. Burroughs. Ed. James Grauerholz. New York: Grove, 2000.

The Letters of William S. Burroughs, 1945–1959. Ed. Oliver Harris. New York: Penguin, 1993.

Letters to Allen Ginsberg, 1953–1957. New York: Full Court, 1982.

My Education: A Book of Dreams. New York: Penguin, 1995.

Naked Lunch: The Restored Text. 1959. Ed. James Grauerholz and Oliver Harris. New York: Grove, 2001.

Naked Scientology/Ali's Smile. Bonn: Expanded Media Editions, 1972.

Nova Express: The Restored Text. 1964. Ed. Oliver Harris. New York: Grove, 2013.

Painting and Guns. Madras, India: Hanuman Books, 1994.

The Place of Dead Roads. New York: Henry Holt, 1983.
Port of Saints. Berkeley, Calif.: Blue Wind, 1973.
Queer: 25th Anniversary Edition. 1985. Ed. Oliver Harris. New York: Penguin, 2010.
Rub Out the Word: The Letters of William S. Burroughs, 1959–1974. Ed. Bill Morgan. New York: HarperCollins, 2012.
The Soft Machine: The Restored Text. Ed. Oliver Harris. 1961. New York: Grove, 2014.
The Ticket That Exploded: The Restored Text. 1962. New York: Grove, 2014.
Tornado Alley. Ann Arbor, Mich.: Cherry Valley, 1989.
The Western Lands. New York: Penguin, 1987.
The Wild Boys: A Book of the Dead. New York: Grove, 1971.
With William Burroughs: A Report from the Bunker. Ed. Victor Bockris. New York: St. Martin's Griffin, 1981.
Word Virus: The William S. Burroughs Reader. Ed. James Grauerholz and Ira Silverberg. New York: Grove, 1998.

Books by William S. Burroughs and Others

With Allen Ginsberg. *The Yage Letters*. San Francisco: City Lights Books, 1963.
———. *The Yage Letters Redux*. Expanded edition of *The Yage Letters*. Ed. Oliver Harris. New York: City Lights, 2006.
With Robert F. Gale. *The Book of Breeething*. Berkeley, Calif.: Blue Wind, 1975.
With Brion Gysin. *The Exterminator*. San Francisco: Dave Hasselwood, 1967.
———. *The Third Mind*. New York: Seaver Books, 1978.
With Brion Gysin, Gregory Corso, and Sinclair Beiles. *Minutes to Go*. San Francisco: City Lights, 1960.
With Brion Gysin and Ian Sommerville. *Let the Mice In*. West Glover, VT: Something Else, 1973.
With Keith Haring. *Apocalypse*. New York: G. Mulder, 1988.
With Jack Kerouac. *And the Hippos Were Boiled in Their Tanks*. New York: Grove, 2008.
With David Odier. *The Job: Interviews with William S. Burroughs*. New York: Penguin, 1969.

Audio Recordings by or Featuring William S. Burroughs

The Black Rider: The Casting of the Magic Bullets. With Tom Waits and Robert Wilson. Island, 1993.
Breakthrough in Grey Room. Sub Rosa, 1992.
Call Me Burroughs. Rhino, 1965.
Dead City Radio. Island Records, 1990.
"Just One Fix." With Ministry. *Psalm 69: Or How to Succeed and Suck Eggs*. Sire, 1992.
"Late Show." With Laurie Anderson. *Home of the Brave*. Warner Brothers, 1986.
The Priest They Called Him. With Kurt Cobain. T/K, 1993.
Spare-Ass Annie and Other Tales. Island, 1993.

Films Featuring, Written by, or about Burroughs

Ah Pook Is Here. Dir. Philip Hunt. 1994.
The Beat Generation: An American Dream. Dir. Janet Forman. Winstar, 1987.
The Beat Hotel. Dir. Alan Govenar. First Run Features, 2012.
Bill and Tony. Dir. Antony Balch. NP, 1972.

Burroughs: The Movie. Dir. Howard Brookner. Criterion, 1983.
The Cut-Ups. Dir. Antony Balch. NP, 1966.
Decoder. Dir. Muscha. Fett Film, 1984.
Drugstore Cowboy. Dir. Gus Van Sant. Avenue Pictures, 1989.
Flicker. Dir. Nik Sheehan. Alive Mind, 2008.
The Junky's Christmas. Dir. Nick Donkin and Melodie McDaniel. Prod. Francis Ford Coppola. Koch Vision, 1993.
Kill Your Darlings. Dir. John Krokidas. Killer Films, 2013.
Naked Lunch. Dir. David Cronenberg. Criterion, 1991.
On the Road. Dir. Walter Salles. MK2 Productions, 2012.
The Source. Dir. Chuck Workman. Fox Lorber, 2000.
Taking Tiger Mountain. Dir. Tom Huckabee and Kent Smith. Players Chess Club, 1983.
Towers Open Fire. Dir. Antony Balch. NP, 1963.
William Buys a Parrot. Dir. Antony Balch. NP, 1963.
William S. Burroughs: A Man Within. Dir. Yony Leyser. Oscilloscope Laboratories, 2010.
William S. Burroughs: Commissioner of Sewers. Dir. Klaus Maeck. NP, 1991.
William S. Burroughs in the Dreamachine. Dir. Aes-Nihil. Cult Epics, 2014.

Secondary Sources

Allmer, Patricia, and John Sears. *Taking Shots: The Photography of William S. Burroughs*. Munich: Prestel, 2014.
Ansen, Alan. *William Burroughs: An Essay*. Sudbury, MA: Water Row, 1986.
Baccolini, Raffaella, and Tom Moylan, eds. *Dark Horizons: Science Fiction and the Dystopian Imagination*. New York: Routledge, 2003.
Baker, Phil. *William S. Burroughs*. London: Reaktion Books, 2010.
Baldwin, Douglas G. "'Word Begets Image and Image Is Virus': Undermining Language and Film in the Works of William S. Burroughs." *College Literature* 27.1 (Winter 2000): 63–83.
Banash, David. "Burroughs Resists Globalization." *Postmodern Culture* 16.2 (2006): 989–1012.
———. "From Advertising to the Avant-Garde: Rethinking the Invention of Collage." *Postmodern Culture* 14.2 (2004): 153–71.
Barrish, Phillip. "Health Policy in Dystopia." *Literature and Medicine* 34.1 (2016): 106–31.
Bennett, Benjamin. "Intransitive Autobiography: *Naked Lunch* and the Problem of Personal Identity." *Art* 24–25 (Fall/Winter 2008): 32–39.
Black, Jack. *You Can't Win*. Blacksburg, VA: Wider, 1926.
Blank, A. R. *My Darling Killer: How Lucien Carr Introduced Jack Kerouac, Allen Ginsberg, and William Burroughs, Killed David Kammerer, and Shaped the Beat Generation*. Lexington, KY: n.p., 2013.
Blasini, Luis. *Blew the Shot: A Story of the Death of Joan Vollmer*. New York: Five Fingered, 2016.
Bockris, Victor. *Beat Punks*. Boston: Da Capo, 2000.
Bolton, Michael Sean. "Getting Off the Point: Deconstructing Context in the Novels of William S. Burroughs." *Journal of Narrative Theory* 40.1 (2010): 53–79.
———. "William S. Burroughs, Michael Serres, and the Word Parasite." *Journal of Beat Studies* 4 (2016): 1–15.

Breu, Christopher. "The Novel Enfleshed: *Naked Lunch* and the Literature of Materiality." *Twentieth-Century Literature* 57.2 (2011): 199–223.

Brodie, Janet Farrell, and Marc Redfield, eds. *High Anxieties: Cultural Studies in Addiction*. Berkeley: University of California Press, 2002.

Bukatman, Scott. *Terminal Identity: The Virtual Subject in Postmodern Science Fiction*. Durham, N.C.: Duke University Press, 1993.

Caveney, Graham. *Gentleman Junkie: The Life and Legacy of William S. Burroughs*. Boston: Little, Brown, 1998.

Campbell, James. *This Is the Beat Generation: San Francisco—New York—Paris*. Berkeley: University of California Press, 1999.

Celeste, Reni. "In the Web with David Cronenberg." *Cineaction* 65 (2004): 2–5.

Charters, Ann, ed. *Beat Down to Your Soul: What Was the Beat Generation?* New York: Penguin, 2001.

———. *The Portable Beat Reader*. New York: Penguin, 1992.

Cline, Kurt. "'Time Junky': Shamanic Journeyings and Gnostic Eschatology in the Novels of William S. Burroughs." *Tamkang Review* 43.2 (June 2013): 33–58.

Collins, Ronald K. L., and David M. Skover. *Mania: The Story of the Outraged and Outrageous Lives That Launched a Cultural Revolution*. Oak Park, IL: Top Five Books, 2013.

Davenport, Stephen. "Queer Shoulders to the Wheel: Beat Movement as Men's Movement." *Journal of Men's Studies* 3.4 (1995): 297–307.

de Man, Paul. *Allegories of Reading: Figurative Language in Rousseau, Nietzsche, Rilke, and Proust*. New Haven, Conn.: Yale University Press, 1979.

Downing, David, and Kim Kerbis. "Exterminate All Rational Thought: David Cronenberg's Filmic Vision of William S. Burroughs's *Naked Lunch*." *Psychoanalytic Review* 85.5 (1998): 775–92.

Eburne, Jonathan Paul. "Trafficking in the Void: Burroughs, Kerouac, and the Consumption of Otherness." *Modern Fiction Studies* 43.1 (1997): 53–92.

Fallows, Collin, and Synne Genzmer, eds. *Cut-Ups, Cut-Ins, Cut-Outs: The Art of William S. Burroughs*. Vienna: Verlag für modern Kunst Nürnberg, 2012.

Fazzino, Jimmy. *World Beats: Beat Generation Writing and the Worlding of U.S. Literature*. Hanover, N.H.: Dartmouth College Press, 2016.

Felver, Christopher. *Beat*. San Francisco: Last Gasp, 2007.

Fielder, Leslie. *Waiting for the End*. New York: Stein and Day, 1964.

Foster, Edward Halsey. *Understanding the Beats*. Columbia: University of South Carolina Press, 1992.

———. *Understanding the Black Mountain Poets*. Columbia: University of South Carolina Press, 1995.

Foucault, Michel. *Discipline and Punish: The Birth of the Prison*. Trans. Alan Sheridan. New York: Vintage, 1975.

Fox, James. "William Burroughs: Return of the Invisible Man." *Rolling Stone*. https://www.rollingstone.com/culture/culture-news/william-burroughs-return-of-the-invisible-man-103343. Accessed April 30, 2019.

Fritz, James. *The Beat Killer: A Biography of Beat Writer Lucien Car and the Riverside Park Murder*. Lexington, KY: Bookcaps, 2012.

Garcia-Robles, Jorge. *The Stray Bullet: William S. Burroughs in Mexico*. Trans. Daniel C. Schechter. Minneapolis: University of Minnesota Press, 2013.

Grace, Nancy M., and Jennie Skerl, eds. *The Transnational Beat Generation.* New York: Palgrave Macmillan, 2012.

Grattan, Sean. "A Grenade with the Fuse Lit: William S. Burroughs and the Retroactive Utopias in *Cities of the Red Night.*" *Utopian Studies* 21.1 (2010): 118–38.

Grauerholz, James. "Afterword." In *And the Hippos Were Boiled in Their Tanks.* By William S. Burroughs and Jack Kerouac, 185–214. New York: Grove, 2008.

Grimstad, Paul C. "Algorithm—Genre—Linguesterie: 'Creative Distortion' in *Count Zero* and *Nova Express.*" *Journal of Modern Literature* 27.4 (Summer 2004): 82–92.

———. "Notes on Burroughs." *Raritan* 36.2 (2016): 52–61.

Halberstam, David. *The Fifties.* New York: Random House, 1993.

Harris, Oliver. "Not Burroughs's Final Fix: Materializing *The Yage Letters.*" *Postmodern Culture* 16.2 (2006): 175–93.

———. "A Response to John Watters, 'The Control Machine: Myth in *The Soft Machine* of W. S. Burroughs.'" *Connotations* 6.3 (1996–97): 337–53.

———. *William Burroughs and the Secret of Fascination.* Carbondale: Southern Illinois University Press, 2003.

Harris, Oliver, and Ian MacFayden, eds. *Naked Lunch@50: Anniversary Essays.* Carbondale: Southern Illinois University Press, 2009.

Harrison, K. C. "Leroi Jones's Radio and the Literary 'Break' from Ellison to Burroughs." *African American Review* 47.2–3 (2014): 357–74.

Heil, Alex, and Ian MacFayden. *William S. Burroughs/Cut.* Cologne, Germany: Verlag der Buchhandlung Walter König, Köln, 2013.

Houen, Alex. "William S. Burroughs's *Cities of the Red Night* Trilogy: Writing Outer Space." *Journal of American Studies* 40.3 (2006): 523–49.

Indiana, Gary. *Utopia's Debris.* New York: Basic Books, 2008.

Jaehne, Karen. "David Cronenberg on William Burroughs: Dead Ringers Do *Naked Lunch.*" *Film Quarterly* 45.3 (Spring 1992): 2–6.

Johnson, Rob. *The Lost Years of William S. Burroughs: Beats in South Texas.* College Station: Texas A&M University Press, 2006.

Johnson, Ronna C., and Nancy M. Grace, eds. *Girls Who Wore Black: Women Writing the Beat Generation.* New Brunswick, N.J.: Rutgers University Press, 2002.

Johnston, Allan. "Consumption, Addiction, Vision, Energy: Political Economies and Utopian Visions in the Writings of the Beat Generation." *College Literature* 32.2 (2005): 103–26.

Kaufmann, Donald L. "The Mailer Legacy and Aleatory Burroughs." *Mailer Review* 6.1 (2012): 318–25.

Knight, Arthur, and Kit Knight, eds. *The Beat Vision.* New York: Paragon House, 1987.

Knight, Brenda, ed. *Women of the Beat Generation: The Writers, Artists, and Muses at the Heart of a Revolution.* Berkeley, Calif.: Conari, 1996.

Lane, Véronique. *The French Genealogy of the Beat Generation: Burroughs, Ginsberg, and Kerouac's Appropriations of Modern Literature, from Rimbaud to Michaux.* New York: Bloomsbury, 2017.

Langeteig, Kendra. "Horror Autotoxicus in the Red Night Trilogy: Ironic Fruits of Burroughs's Terminal Vision." *Configurations* 5.1 (1997): 135–69.

Loewinsohn, Ron. "'Gentle Reader, I Fain Would Spare You This, but My Pen Hath Its Will Like the Ancient Mariner': Narrator(s) and Audience in William S. Burroughs's *Naked Lunch.*" *Contemporary Literature* 39.4 (1998): 560–98.

Loranger, Carol. "'This Book Spill Off the Page in All Directions': What Is the Text of *Naked Lunch?*" *Postmodern Culture* 10.1 (1999): 145–74.

Loydell, Rupert. *My Kind of Angel: I.M. William Burroughs*. Exeter, U.K.: Stride, 1998.

Lyndenberg, Robin. *Word Cultures: Radical Theory and Practice in William S. Burroughs' Fiction*. Urbana: University of Illinois Press, 1987.

McCaffery, Larry, ed. *Storming the Reality Studio: A Casebook of Cyberpunk and Postmodern Science Fiction*. Durham, N.C.: Duke University Press, 1991.

McNeill, Malcolm. *The Lost Art of Ah Pook Is Here: Images from the Graphic Novel*. Seattle: Fantagraphics Books, 2012.

———. *Observed While Falling: Bill Burroughs, Ah Pook, and Me*. Seattle: Fantagraphics Books, 2012.

Meyer, Christopher. "The Psychopharmacology of Everyday Life: W. S. Burroughs and the Narcotic Regime." *American Journal of Semiotics* 9.2–3 (1992): 167–84.

Miles, Barry. *The Beat Hotel: Ginsberg, Burroughs, and Corso in Paris, 1957–1963*. New York: Grove: 2000.

———. *Call Me Burroughs: A Life*. New York: Twelve, 2013.

———. *William Burroughs: El Hombre Invisible*. London: Virgin Books, 1992.

Moore, Nathan. "Nova Law: William S. Burroughs and the Logic of Control." *Law and Literature* 19.3 (2007): 435–70.

Morgan, Bill. *Beat Atlas: A State by State Guide to the Beat Generation in America*. San Francisco: City Lights, 2011.

———. *The Beat Generation in New York: A Walking Tour of Jack Kerouac's City*. San Francisco: City Lights Books, 1997.

———. *The Beat Generation in San Francisco: A Literary Tour*. San Francisco: City Lights, 2003.

———. *The Beats Abroad: A Global Guide to the Beat Generation*. San Francisco: City Lights, 2016.

———. *The Typewriter Is Holy: The Complete, Uncensored History of the Beat Generation*. Berkeley, Calif.: Counterpoint, 2010.

Morgan, Ted. *Literary Outlaw: The Life and Times of William S. Burroughs*. New York: Avon Books, 1988.

Mortenson, Erik. "Turkish Censorship, Cultural Translation, and the Trial of William S. Burroughs's *The Soft Machine*." *Arizona Quarterly* 72.3 (2016): 47–73.

Mottram, Eric. *William Burroughs: The Algebra of Need*. London: Marion Boyars, 1977.

Mullins, Greg. *Colonial Affairs: Bowles, Burroughs, and Chester Write Tangier*. Madison: University of Wisconsin Press, 2002.

Muñoz, José Esteban. *Cruising Utopia: The Then and There of Queer Futurity*. New York: New York University Press, 2009.

Murphy, Timothy S. "Intersection Points: Teaching William S. Burroughs's *Naked Lunch*." *College Literature* 27.1 (2000): 84–102.

———. *Wising Up the Marks: The Amodern William Burroughs*. Berkeley: University of California Press, 1997.

Nealon, Jeffrey T. "'Junk' and the Other: Burroughs and Levinas on Drugs." *Postmodern Culture* 6.1 (1995): n.p.

Nietzsche, Friedrich. *Beyond Good and Evil*. Translated by Walter Kaufmann. New York: Random House, 1966.

Paton, Fiona. “Monstrous Rhetoric: *Naked Lunch,* National Insecurity, and Gothic Files.” *Texas Studies in Language and Literature* 52.1 (Spring 2010): 48–69.

Plimpton, George, ed. *Beat Writers at Work: The Paris Review.* New York: Modern Library, 1999.

Porush, David. *The Soft Machine: Cybernetic Fiction.* New York: Methuen, 1985.

Punday, Daniel. “Narrative after Deconstruction: Structure and the Negative Poetics of William Burroughs’s *Cities of the Red Night.*” *Style* 29.1 (Spring 1995): 36–57.

———. “Word Dust: William Burroughs’s Multimedia Studies.” *Mosaic* 40.3 (2007): 33–49.

Punter, David. “William Burroughs: The Scene of Addiction.” *Gothic Studies* 11.2 (2009): 74–82.

Reality Studio: A William S. Burroughs Community. Supervert, 2018. https://realitystudio.org/. Accessed April 30, 2019.

Rose, Barbara. “Cultural Paranoia, Conspiracy Plots, and the American Ideology: William Burroughs’s *Cities of the Red Night.*” *Canadian Review of American Studies* 29.2 (1999): 89–111.

Russell, Jamie. *Queer Burroughs.* New York: Palgrave, 2001.

Sargeant, Jack. *Naked Lens: Beat Cinema.* Berkeley, Calif.: Soft Skull, 2008.

Savran, David. *Taking It Like a Man: White Masculinity, Masochism, and Contemporary American Culture.* Princeton, N.J.: Princeton University Press, 1998.

Schneiderman, Davis, and Philip Walsh, eds. *Retaking the Universe: William S. Burroughs in the Age of Globalization.* London: Pluto, 2004.

Schroeder, Randy. “Inheriting Chaos: Burroughs, Pynchon, Sterling, Rucker.” *Extrapolation* 43.1 (2002): 89–97.

Shenasha, Mitch. *The Occult William S. Burroughs.* Amazon Digital Services, 2013.

Shoaf, Eric C. *William S. Burroughs: A Collector’s Guide.* Providence, RI: Inkblot, 2014.

Silverberg, Ira. *Everything Is Permitted: The Making of Naked Lunch.* New York: Grove Weidenfeld, 1992.

Skerl, Jennie. *William S. Burroughs.* Boston: Twayne, 1985.

Sobieszek, Robert A. *Ports of Entry: William S. Burroughs and the Arts.* Los Angeles: Los Angeles County Museum of Art, 1996.

Sondergard, Sid. “Unable to Queer the Deal: William S. Burroughs’s Negotiations with ‘Eugene Allerton.’” *Critique* 44.2 (2003): 144–56.

Spann, Michael. *William S. Burroughs’ Unforgettable Characters: Lola “La Chata” and Bernabé Jurando.* Brisbane: Inkblot, 2013.

Stephenson, Gregory. *The Daybreak Boys: Essays on the Literature of the Beat Generation.* Carbondale: Southern Illinois University Press, 1990.

Sterritt, David. *The Beats: A Very Short Introduction.* Oxford: Oxford University Press, 2013.

———. *Mad to Be Saved: The Beats, The ’50s, and Film.* Carbondale: Southern Illinois University Press, 1998.

Stevens, Matthew Levi. *The Magical Universe of William S. Burroughs.* Oxford: Mandrake of Oxford, 2014.

Strand, Eric. “The Last Frontier: Burroughs’s Early Work and International Tourism.” *Twentieth-Century Literature* 59.1 (2013): 1–36.

Tabbi, Joseph. *Postmodern Sublime: Technology and American Writing from Mailer to Cyberpunk.* Ithaca, N.Y.: Cornell University Press, 1996.

Tietchen, Todd. "Language Out of Language: Excavating the Roots of Cultural Jamming and Postmodern Activism from William S. Burroughs' *Nova* Trilogy." *Discourse* 23.3 (2001): 107–32.

Tyell, John. *Naked Angels: Kerouac, Ginsberg, Burroughs.* Chicago: Ivan R. Dee, 1976.

Vale, V. *Re/Search 4/5: William S. Burroughs, Brion Gysin, and Throbbing Gristle.* Monroe, n.p., 1982.

Vanderheide, John. "The Apocatastasis of Community in Late Burroughs." *Arcadia* 43.1 (2008): 63–77.

Waldman, Anne, ed. *The Beat Book: Writings from the Beat Generation.* Boston: Shambhala, 1996.

Waldman, Anne, and Laura Wright, eds. *Beats at Naropa: An Anthology.* Minneapolis: Coffee House, 2009.

Watters, John G. "The Control Machine: Myth in *The Soft Machine* of W. S. Burroughs." *Connotations* 5.2–3 (1995–96): 284–303.

Weidner, Chad. *The Green Ghost: William Burroughs and the Ecological Mind.* Carbondale: Southern Illinois University Press, 2016.

Weiss, William. *Orbiting William S. Burroughs.* Amazon Digital Services, 2005.

Wermer-Colan, Alex. "Implicating the Confessor: The Autobiographical Ploy in William S. Burroughs's Early Work." *Twentieth-Century Literature* 56.4 (2010): 493–529.

White, J. M. *Naropa Journals: William Burroughs, Allen Ginsberg, and the Beat Revolution.* Brush Creek, RI:: Anomolaic, 2015.

Whiting, Frederick. "Monstrosity on Trial: The Case of *Naked Lunch.*" *Twentieth Century Literature* 52.2 (2006): 145–74.

Wild, Paul H. "William S. Burroughs and the Maya Gods of Death: The Uses of Archaeology." *College Literature* 35.1 (2008): 38–57.

Wills, David S. *Scientologist! William S. Burroughs and the "Weird Cult."* United Kingdom: Beatdom Books, 2013.

Wilson, Meagan. "Your Reputation Precedes You: A Reception Study of *Naked Lunch.*" *Journal of Modern Literature* 35.2 (2012) 98–125.

Wood, Brent. "Bring the Noise!: William S. Burroughs and Music in the Expanded Field." *Postmodern Culture* 5.2 (1995): n.p.

———. "William S. Burroughs and the Language of Cyberpunk." *Science Fiction Studies* 23.1 (1996): 1–20.

Yu, Timothy. "Oriental Cities, Postmodern Futures: *Naked Lunch, Blade Runner,* and *Neuromancer. MELUS* 33.4 (2008): 45–71.

INDEX